MINUTES TO MIDNIGHT
TWELVE ESSAYS ON WATCHMEN

MINUTES TO MIDNIGHT
TWELVE ESSAYS ON WATCHMEN

edited by

Richard Bensam

SEQUART RESEARCH & LITERACY ORGANIZATION   EDWARDSVILLE, ILLINOIS

Minutes to Midnight: Twelve Essays on Watchmen
Edited by Richard Bensam

Revised first edition, November 2011, ISBN 978-1-4663-5089-2. First edition, October 2010.

Cover by Kevin Colden. Design by Julian Darius. Interior art is © DC Comics; please visit dccomics.com.

Published by Sequart Research & Literacy Organization. Edited by Richard Bensam.

For more information about other titles in this series, visit Sequart.org/books.

Contents

Obsolete Models a Specialty: An Introduction

by Richard Bensam

The British comics artist and comics historian Steve Whitaker once described a conversation he had with Dave Gibbons at a comics convention in the fall of 1986, sometime not long after the fourth issue of *Watchmen* was published. Whitaker had been following the series very closely, of course, and as a careful reader believed he had discovered the key to the story. So when he ran into Gibbons at the convention, he asked the *Watchmen* artist, "Rorschach is the real center of the story, isn't he? He's the character we should be keeping our eyes on, the one everything else revolves around, right?"

As Whitaker told it, Gibbons shook his head and replied, "That's not it. There isn't meant to be one central character. The whole point is that everyone gets to choose the character they want to follow. It could be Rorschach or the Comedian or Ozymandias. *You* could be Nite Owl." Retelling the story later, Whitaker claimed he was never entirely sure if the *Watchmen* artist had compared him to Nite Owl because he saw something of Dan Dreiberg's personality traits in Whitaker... or if this was Dave's tactful way of hinting that Steve was putting on weight.

That question may never be answered, but I've often thought about that anecdote in the years since then... not least because Nite Owl was always my guy as well. In fact, I always imagined he was the overlooked central character in *Watchmen*.

It's true that Nite Owl doesn't narrate his own life story over the course of an issue, as the other living heroes in *Watchmen* do. Nor do we see him extensively in the recollections of others, as we do with the late Comedian. From his lack of prominence in the stories recounted by the other leads, Dan Dreiberg's most distinguishing trait seems to have been that most of the other costumed heroes didn't have any strong feelings about him one way or the other. And yet, he's the one who makes the resolution possible by deciding to free Rorschach from prison; he's the one who does the research that ultimately discloses their real adversary; and he's the one who gets the girl and lives happily ever after. That list of accomplishments certainly befits "the hero of the story," wouldn't you think?

But there's another reason for Nite Owl to hold our attention, and it takes us back to the above anecdote and leads us directly to the point of this whole book. Consider:

The first thing we learn about Nite Owl in the first issue of *Watchmen* is that he idolizes the masked heroes of a previous era. He has a home full of costumes, accessories, memorabilia, and collectibles. The very thing that gives his life meaning is something he often feels embarrassed about. He needs to keep it secret and hidden or risk harassment and humiliation. Being able to admit his feelings at last to other people who share his interests comes as a profound relief. When he becomes friends with the man whose exploits inspired him and is briefly able to follow in his footsteps, he's over the moon. Let's face it – if they held conventions of costumed hero enthusiasts in the world of *Watchmen*, Daniel Dreiberg would happily attend. If some toy company had issued action figures of the Minutemen, Daniel would have the complete set on display in a glass case somewhere in his Manhattan townhouse.

In other words, Dan Dreiberg is the perfect analog of a comics fan. His friendship with Hollis Mason is much like that of a fan who corresponds with and befriends his or her favorite creators. Hollis can certainly be considered the "creator" of his Golden Age costumed identity as the original Nite Owl. Extending that analogy slightly further, we might even say Dreiberg's fandom takes the form of wishing to create his own exploits – also very much the case in comics fandom, where many fans aspire to become pros.

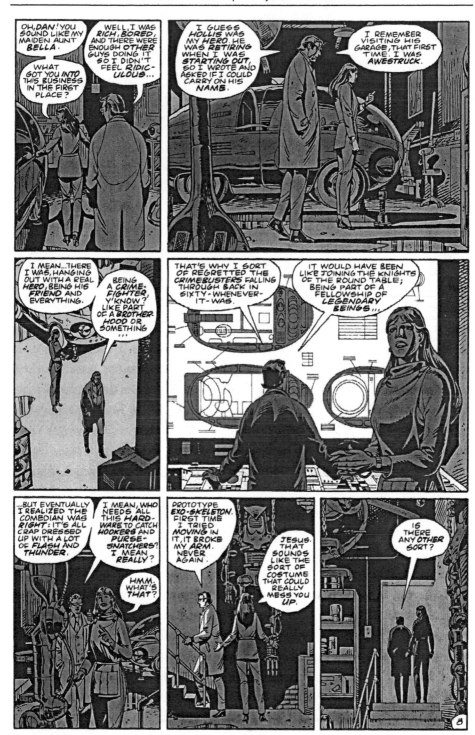

Archetypal fan Daniel Dreiberg shows Laurie Juspeczyk his collectibles and souvenirs. From *Watchmen* #7 (March 1987). Copyright © DC Comics.

Taking all of this into account, Nite Owl would inevitably seem to be the natural viewpoint character for a comics reader – the ideal audience surrogate, our perfect window into the events of *Watchmen*. He's the devoted fan who loved costumed heroes and wanted to live in that world and finally did, only to find himself unfulfilled and let down. Doesn't this dilemma cut right to the goal of *Watchmen* bringing a more mature and sophisticated outlook to bear on the nostalgia-drenched trappings of super-hero comics?

That's how it's always seemed to me. So imagine my consternation if a student of the history and philosophy of science were to say that the real goal of *Watchmen* is the illustration of post-Einsteinian physics as literary metaphor, and therefore Doctor Manhattan is obviously the central figure and most important character in the story.

We're both right, of course. But you'd also be right if you said *Watchmen* was *really* all about using the super-hero genre to satirize the arrogance of American foreign policy and that the Comedian was the pivotal character. Or if you argued Silk Spectre was the real viewpoint character – the sole relatively balanced and normal person among damaged personalities, bent and twisted in various ways by the super-hero concept; the one who shows us how disturbing and neurotic it all looks when you take a step back and see the bigger picture. Or if you said Ozymandias represents us when he sits in front of his wall of television screens – seeking hidden meanings in brightly colored images while his eyes dart constantly from rectangular frame to rectangular frame, feeling himself above everyone else as he tries to discern the end of the story. Remind you of anything?

These answers (and many others besides) are all equally correct. One can even imagine these answers forming the basis of some sort of personality test, something along the lines of asking someone to name his or her favorite Beatle and using that selection to discern something fundamental about that person's outlook. But in *Watchmen,* these different viewpoints mean something more than a Rorschach blot, if you will, or a chance to play "Choose Your Own Adventure." The fact that there are so many different possible interpretations is the whole point; it's not which one you choose that matters, it's that you have the choice. As Jon Osterman would tell you, there is no privileged frame of reference, no one "right" way to look at the universe. Everything is only relative to everything else. This is precisely what Dave Gibbons was saying back in 1986. And in an interview with George Khoury for the career-spanning

overview *The Extraordinary Works of Alan Moore* in 2002, *Watchmen* writer
Alan Moore answered the same question in much the same way:

> *Is Rorschach the protagonist of the book?*
>
> No, I don't think there is a center of the book. I mean, part of what
> *Watchmen* was about is that all of the characters have got very, very
> distinctive views of the world. They've all got very distinctive views of the
> world, but they're all completely different... Ultimately[,] it's the reader
> who has to make the choice. It's the reader's decision, it's the reader's
> world, ultimately, as I say in the last panel, I leave it entirely in your hands.
> That it's up to the reader to formulate their own response to the world –
> sort of – and not to be told what to do by a super-hero or a political leader
> or a comic-book writer, for that matter. I think that was the thinking
> behind *Watchmen*.

So then: the book you now hold is a collection of possible viewpoints on
Watchmen. Different ways to read *Watchmen*, if you will. *Watchmen* as a
carefully constructed murder mystery. *Watchmen* as a formalist experiment in
symmetry. *Watchmen* as postmodern revisionism. *Watchmen* as satire and
homage to prior comics art. *Watchmen* as an inspiration for other media. As
both Dave Gibbons and Alan Moore have said, *Watchmen* is about viewing the
world through more than one filter. This book is about viewing *Watchmen*
through more than one filter. No one perspective is meant to be authoritative
or the last word on the subject, but each one offers an angle you might never
have thought of before.

These perspectives come from a group of immensely talented writers –
some of them veterans with other books and many published essays to their
credit, others at the start of their careers and just on the verge of getting the
attention they deserve.

One common trait among our contributors is that most of them are prolific
online writers, whether on their own personal blogs, or as columnists for one or
another of the news and opinion websites devoted to comics. Even though the
World Wide Web was still five years in the future when *Watchmen* appeared,
there were already comics discussion groups emerging on electronic bulletin
boards, mailing lists, and Usenet newsgroups... and yet, after all this time, we're
still in the process of figuring out how the online world will change the role of
writers. I don't have many answers there, but one thing I can say is that online
writing takes place under the most unrelenting form of competitive pressure
possible – the constant competition for attention. If you're not entertaining or
interesting or informative, the audience goes away. There's just too much else

waiting to distract them. Scheherazade couldn't have had it any worse; in *The Thousand and One Nights*, she only had to entertain one Persian king. In some respects, online writing is as demanding a training ground as a writer could want; it might not help a writer develop a lot of polish, but it demands that writers learn to be lively and engaging.

To my regret as editor, we couldn't fit in even a fraction of the writers who deserve to be here. If Sequart published a twelve *volume* collection of essays on *Watchmen*, each volume the same length as this book, we couldn't include more than a sample of the interesting commentary on *Watchmen* to be found online.

Dedication

Finally, this collection is dedicated to the memory of Dick Giordano, who died on 27 March 2010 at the age of 77.

As the Editor in Chief at Charlton Comics in 1965, Giordano guided the creation of the "Action Hero" line of comics, including updated versions of earlier Charlton characters Captain Atom and Blue Beetle as well as new costumed heroes such as the Question, the Peacemaker, Judomaster, Son of Vulcan, and Nightshade. (You'll read more about several of those characters in the pages that follow.) Featuring stories and artwork by outstanding creators including Steve Ditko, Jim Aparo, Frank McLaughlin, Denny O'Neil, Pete Morisi, Pat Boyette, Joe Gill, and many others, the "Action Hero" titles earned fan acclaim and a devoted cult following but were never a commercial success. All were cancelled before Giordano left the company in 1968.

After becoming Vice President / Executive Editor at DC Comics in 1980, Dick Giordano helped recruit promising British newcomer Alan Moore for his first work in American comics. Giordano was also responsible for DC acquiring the Charlton Action Hero characters after his former employer went out of business. When Moore submitted a proposal for a series using those same Action Heroes in a thoroughly modern story that would push beyond the boundaries of anything seen before in a super-hero comic, Giordano suggested that Moore instead create a new set of characters who would better serve his story. When Giordano approved a request from artist Dave Gibbons to collaborate with Moore on the new project, all these threads converged. Put simply, there would never have been any such thing as *Watchmen* without Dick Giordano.

All of us who enjoyed his work as an artist and editor owe Dick Giordano a debt of gratitude. This is especially true for those of us who were inspired to create our own stories, our own artwork... or even essays about a comic book series he helped publish 25 years ago.

Reassembling the Components in the Correct Sequence: Why You Shouldn't Read *Watchmen* First

by Walter Hudsick

When *Time* magazine named *Watchmen* to their list of "the 100 best English-language novels from 1923 to the present," a whole new audience, feeling there must be something to this comics stuff after all, decided it had to read *Watchmen* to understand comics. If you were one of those people, you were far from alone. In the year 2007, *Watchmen* sold roughly 100,000 copies – an impressive figure some 20 years after its original release. But during the year following the July 2008 debut of the *Watchmen* film trailer, the print version sold over 900,000 copies and spent an unbroken 11 months as the top-selling U.S. graphic novel. *Watchmen* ended up in the hands of a lot of readers who weren't already buying comics, including some who may never have read a single comic before.

Even if you weren't one of those customers, you might have borrowed a copy from a longtime fan; they probably thought it a great service to lend it to you. If so, that well-intentioned generosity may have been ill-advised. Reading *Watchmen* is not your best introduction to the comics idiom. Unless you're a comics fan, you won't have the fluency in the comics form and familiarity with the super-hero genre required to unlock the story's hidden messages. Why, you probably don't even know who the characters really are.

To begin with, Rorschach, Nite Owl, Ozymandias, Dr. Manhattan, and the rest didn't spring full-blown onto the pages of *Watchmen*. In fact, they were mere imitations of the original protagonists of the story – characters created decades earlier at another comics company altogether. As any longtime comics fan will tell you, the secret history of *Watchmen* begins with a minor publishing firm hidden away in the town of Derby, Connecticut.

Charlton Comics had been around since the mid-Forties, always a contender but never a champ in the comics tournament. By the end of the Sixties, super-hero comics publishing would eventually boil down to a competition between the Big Two: old, conservative DC Comics (who had had the good fortune to publish Superman in 1938 and Batman in 1939) and exciting upstart Marvel Comics (successor to the pre-war publisher Timely Comics, home of Captain America), which in the Sixties was bursting with new characters such as the Fantastic Four, the Incredible Hulk, and Spider-Man. The renewed interest in super-heroes that fueled their second ascendance in the late Fifties and early Sixties created a tide that lifted all boats, so Charlton tasked artist and editor Dick Giordano with developing a line of costumed heroes. While Charlton's "Action Heroes" never achieved the popularity of the various super-people over at the Big Two, the characters weren't by any means obscure; some fine talent worked on the books and their stable of characters was familiar to any fan of the time.

The company's premiere hero was Captain Atom (first appearing in Charlton's *Space Adventures* #33, March 1960), co-created by Steve Ditko shortly before he began working on Spider-Man at Marvel. As his name suggested, Captain Atom was a hero with nuclear-based powers. A military scientist is trapped in a newly-designed rocket on a test flight and completely disintegrated; he somehow manages to pull himself together and re-integrate his atomized form, complete with astonishing powers. Well, astonishing if you had never read comics before: he could fly, was really strong and tough, and could fire energy blasts. Continuing his service to the government, the Captain fought typical Cold War villains, aliens, and mad scientists.

In terms of publishing history, the first Charlton hero might be the Blue Beetle. In the early Fifties, during a comics business downturn, Charlton

SPACE ADVENTURES

Astronaut Allen Adam manages to pull himself together in this scene from the debut of Captain Atom in *Space Adventures* #33 (March 1960) by Joe Gill and Steve Ditko. Copyright © DC Comics.

acquired characters from various other defunct companies. One of these was the Blue Beetle, a rookie police patrolman turned Shadow-like detective, courtesy of a bulletproof business suit and some super-strength vitamins. He was first revised in the Fifties as a more straight-forward costumed super-hero, with super-powers granted by a magic scarab he had discovered in his civilian identity as an archaeologist. In 1966, the pages of *Captain Atom* introduced still another hero called Blue Beetle, this one created by Steve Ditko upon his return to Charlton, having been lured back by the offer of greater credit and creative freedom. The new Blue Beetle had a more modern costume and methods, but readers soon learned how the previous Blue Beetle had passed on his name and tradition to his former student. Unfortunately, the brash young inventor lost the scarab in a mishap and had to make do with scientific apparatus of his own devising. In addition to a flash-gun and grappling wires, this new Blue Beetle had his own personal transport – a spheroid flying craft called the Bug – which could hover and from which Beetle would swing on cables.

When this version of the Blue Beetle was in turn promoted to his own series, the pages of *Blue Beetle* #1 introduced yet another new Ditko-created hero. The Question sprang from the same inkwell as Spider-Man, but represented Ditko's own political and philosophical persuasions much more accurately than Marvel's friendly neighborhood wall-crawler or Charlton's less-famous blue bug. The Question – prosaically clad in a business suit, overcoat, and fedora hat, with a mask of "pseudoderm" giving him a completely faceless appearance – was an uncompromising vigilante with no soft spot for criminals, whether in costume or in his real identity as a firebrand television newsman. He was perfectly willing to use physical force to achieve his ends, insisted on personal responsibility and the acceptance of consequences for one's actions, and was not averse to letting criminals die as a result of their own bad choices.

A lesser light of the Charlton crew was *Peter Cannon... Thunderbolt*. When the child of American medical workers in central Asia is orphaned by an epidemic, the boy is taken in by a Tibetan lamasery and trained with the aid of secret scrolls to achieve human perfection. He returns to America to live a life of contemplation and grace – whenever he isn't fighting crime. Created by writer-artist Pete Morisi, then an active police officer, *Peter Cannon... Thunderbolt* was signed merely with the initials "P.A.M." to prevent his NYPD superiors from discovering his moonlighting.

One of Charlton's more confounding heroes was the Peacemaker, billed as "the man who loves peace so much he is willing to fight for it." No, really. A career diplomat in his normal identity, the Peacemaker would don his costume and helmet whenever negotiations, foreign aid arrangements, and bilateral talks slowed down. Usually working covertly, he would shoot, punch, and pummel soldiers, henchmen, and heads of state to ensure peace. Somewhat of a walking contradiction, this hero of harmony lasted for five issues, created by writer Joe Gill and artist Pat Boyette.

Sales on the Action Heroes line proved disappointing, and the comics were cancelled in 1967. Dick Giordano moved on to work at DC Comics, recruiting many of his former Charlton creators to join him there. Meanwhile, Charlton survived by publishing mainly cartoon and television tie-in comics (such as *The Six Million Dollar Man*) before folding in 1986. By that time, the reputation of the Action Heroes had grown, partly due to the involvement of esteemed figures such as Giordano and Ditko, the latter regarded as a seminal American comics creator. But even so, after 18 years of absence, the Action Heroes seemed destined to vanish into obscurity.

Let's review the line-up: a scientist caught in an atomic accident who gains superhuman powers, yet retains his association with the government; a rich guy who uses scientific equipment to follow in the footsteps of an earlier hero of the same name; a brutal vigilante with an uncompromising social philosophy and a completely obscured face; a man of refined tastes whose exceptional talents are the result of years of training and reflection; and a costumed avatar of political irony, a government operative whose name belies his brutal methods and attitudes. Sound familiar?

Of course, there's one more costumed lead in *Watchmen* – Silk Spectre, who is actually the second of two women in the story to wear that name. There is no precise analogue to Silk Spectre in the Charlton stable. The most apt would be Nightshade, a female hero with shadow-based powers who served as a partner of Captain Atom for some time. While that association may bring to mind the relationship between Dr. Manhattan and Silk Spectre, the characters are not very similar otherwise. But don't let that fool you – the overall correlation was there and was deliberate. And what's more, fans knew it.

As Charlton Comics approached its final days, DC Comics Vice-President Paul Levitz purchased the rights to the Action Heroes characters and offered them to Giordano, knowing how much they had meant to the editor. Alan

Moore, a Brit who had only recently begun writing for American comics, then pitched a story premise to Giordano: Moore wanted to take these super-hero characters and place them in a grimmer, more realistic milieu and turn the whole genre on its head.

Moore had originally devised this story around yet another stable of defunct super-heroes from a publisher called MLJ, better known as the publishers of Archie comics. When he realized that the Charlton characters were available as potential toys in his sandbox, Moore grafted the idea onto them because, as he said in a later interview, "it didn't matter which super-heroes it was about, as long as the characters had some kind of emotional resonance, that people would recognize them, so it would have the shock and surprise value."

The intention of *Watchmen* from the very beginning was not merely to present a general revisionist spin on the super-hero genre but to take specific characters that the readers knew (and perhaps cared about) and twist them around. The automatic recognition of the heroes was part of the plan for how the piece would work; without that implicit understanding from the reader, the connection necessary to carry the impact of the story isn't there.

As it turned out, DC had plans to use some of the Charlton characters in their own stories, relocating them, as it were, to the same universe with Superman and Batman. Since *Watchmen* would do things with – and to – the characters that would render them unsuitable for subsequent use in mainstream comics, Giordano vetoed the idea of using Captain Atom *et al*. But he liked the project concept and encouraged Moore to restructure it with newly-created characters. Moore just recreated the Charlton heroes – intentionally, specially, and precisely so that they would be recognized as such.

When Dr. Manhattan zaps Viet Cong troops into oblivion with a gesture, we're meant to recall Captain Atom trading power blasts with Commie super-villains, suddenly given real historical and political context. When Nite Owl flies over the city in his google-eyed craft Archie, we're supposed to see Blue Beetle in his flying Bug, now hobbled by insecurity and sexual dysfunction. When the uncompromising Rorschach lectures on morality, we hear the Question holding forth, except now the voice of a sociopathic loner replaces that of a crusading TV reporter. When Ozymandias takes down an assassin or defeats a crime boss through his physical and mental discipline, we're meant to recognize the martial arts training of Peter Cannon, only with his indomitable self-confidence turned to messianic conceit. And when the Comedian murders a pregnant woman in a rage, we're supposed to understand just how incongruous and untenable the Peacemaker's persona and philosophy really were.

In Silk Spectre, we didn't see very much of Nightshade. Instead, we saw Phantom Lady (a character from the Quality Comics line of the 1940s) and Black Canary (a DC character of similar vintage), both of whom had had origins almost as old as comics themselves and experienced a later revamp – just like Silk Spectre. Whether this disparate treatment of the only significant female hero in *Watchmen* is meta-commentary on the marginalization of female super-heroes or is merely another example of that marginalization is for the individual reader to decide.

In any case, the lack of clear correspondence with the one super-heroine did not collapse the conceit; any comics reader worth his salt merely had to squint at the pages of *Watchmen* to see the Charlton heroes move through the story. Everyone knew that the story had originally been planned for the Charlton heroes; Giordano had revealed as much even before publication, and the fan press of the mid-Eighties was well aware of the connection. This connection was easy for readers to make and had its intended effect. The impact was like tuning into *Bonanza* to find Hoss and Little Joe pistol-whipping a traveling salesman – or watching Wally and the Beaver do a line of coke in the clubhouse during *Leave It To Beaver*. For all its considerable merits as narrative, art, and social commentary, without this intertextuality, this familiarity with these specific characters, the power of the piece is diminished, and arguably, the artist's plan is unfulfilled.

You may wave this consideration away, citing the power of Moore's writing and Gibbons's art to create wholly actualized characters compelling in their own right, and you may have a point: a work of art can easily outstrip or veer away from creator intent. But there's something else besides direct correlation to Charlton informing *Watchmen*, and unless you were a fan, you probably weren't there for the glimpses into the alternative treatment of the genre that came before *Watchmen*. You may not have seen the brief lightning flashes showing that it was possible to think critically about this super-hero stuff long before Rorschach murmured his first "hurm" – flashes that continue to illuminate the horizon and cast shadows on any reading of *Watchmen*. You have likely never read "Superduperman!" or "Man of Steel, Woman of Kleenex" or *Super-Folks*, and you should.

"Superduperman!" appeared in *Mad* when comic-book parodies were its stock in trade. Before the Comics Code Authority was established in the Fifties and fundamentally changed everything about comics publishing, *Mad* was more like a regular comic book than the magazine it has long been. Part of the E.C. Comics line, it was a humor publication, unlike the horror and crime books that comprised most of the company's output, and it printed both funny comic strips and parodies of other comic books – such as "Superduperman!", in the April 1953 issue. This strip, written by Harvey Kurtzman and drawn by Wally Wood, presented both metacommentary on the comics industry and insight into the disturbing psychosexuality of costumed super-heroes in that typically anarchic *Mad* style. This was six months before Alan Moore was born.

The story presents a battle between the Superman parody Superduperman (depicted as an oafish muscle-bound poser) and the opportunistic Captain Marbles (representing Superman's most popular competitor, Captain Marvel). The two, neither very sympathetic, pummel each other for most of the strip's eight pages, paralleling the legal battle that the publishers of the two original characters had been engaged in for almost 12 years over copyright infringement. Like the lawsuit, the comic-book battle ends with a Super-win and the Captain being sentenced to oblivion. Comics characters being used to comment on the comics field in a comic book? How *Watchmen* of *Mad*!

Even more deconstructionist than the obvious parallel to the lawsuit of the heroes was the story's depiction of the relationship between Clark Bent and Lois Pain. Clark's sniveling, submissive sycophant, begging for a sniff of haughty Lois's perfume and accepting both verbal and physical abuse for his trouble, focused a spotlight on the ever-problematic triangle between Superman, Lois Lane, and Clark Kent. With just a little judicious exaggeration, the idea of an almost all-powerful figure voluntary disguising himself as a mild-mannered man and then pining for an uninterested woman suddenly seemed a little, well, dysfunctional. Kurtzman and Wood were not deliberately setting out to examine and map these deviant corners of super-hero sexuality in the same way that Moore would decades later; nonetheless, the journey of exploration is clearly underway.

This issue of super-sexuality was covered much more directly in the essay "Man of Steel, Woman of Kleenex" by Larry Niven, first appearing in his 1971 collection *All the Myriad Ways*. In it, the science-fiction author speculates on the possibility and consequences of a sexual relationship between Superman and a human woman. In the midst of humorous (and often puerile) conjectures about the danger of a super-ejaculation and the nature of super-sperm, Niven raises a serious question: how likely is it that an extra-terrestrial would find an Earthling sexually attractive anyway? There is a direct line from this analysis of Superman's sexual desires to the contemplation of Dr. Manhattan's two-party *ménage a trois* in Watchmen: Zeus notwithstanding, would gods really want – or even be able – to sleep with humans?

But these two isolated pieces are just throwaways, right? A parody comic strip in a juvenile humor magazine and a bit of critical ephemera in a sci-fi anthology may have raised some interesting points, but they don't really count: *Watchmen* can still be called the first actual sustained treatment of "realistic" super-heroes. Well, sure. Except for a novel published in 1977.

Robert Mayer's *Super-Folks* was a long-form, multi-layered literary effort, functioning simultaneously as a comic farce, a commentary on current affairs, and an examination of the super-hero motif. A *roman à clef* featuring analogues of Superman, Captain Marvel, and other comic-book heroes (with undisguised appearances by Peter Pan and other pop culture characters), it contains deft pastiches of many of the narrative conventions of super-hero comics. The story elements themselves include a plot to kill heroes, a hero coming out of retirement, deviant sexuality, and an antagonist who heads a global conglomerate.

Sounds familiar, doesn't it? The book was never very successful, either in its first incarnation or in a special comics-culture reprint on its 25th anniversary, complete with a new introduction by comics writer Kurt Busiek, who recounts its specific influence on later works. But those who were really connected to comics had passed it around when it first came out, and when *Watchmen* showed up a few years later, they could hear the echoes clearly. But if you haven't read Mayer's novel... or Niven's essay... or Kurtzman and Wood's story... you won't hear any of these echoes. Another layer of appreciation – the understanding that Watchmen stands not as *sui generis*, the first new look at the super-hero genre, but rather as one work in a lineage of serious and frivolous efforts to explore the same themes – will be absent.

Maybe that's okay. You won't get all the nuances, you won't feel the historicity of each observation, and you won't see the shadows lined up behind each image. You can still read *Watchman* as a story of these particular characters doing their own particular thing in their own particular way, without specific background knowledge.

Well, if you're not a comic-book fan (or more specifically, a super-hero comics fan), there's another barrier to access. And by fan, we don't just mean someone who read Superman, Batman, or Spider-Man as a kid, even if they still read the funnies, Cathy or Garfield or Dilbert, in the local newspaper. We're talking about people who have spent big chunks of their lives devoted to following super-hero stories; who have referred to the genre as a "mythos" with a straight face; who have wondered at length whether the Hulk or Superman was stronger, argued with someone else about it, fought about it, and then been thrilled when the meeting finally took place. (Knowing, as only such a person would, that the chance of Hulk and Superman meeting was remote because two different companies publish the two characters.) But without some baseline context that comes from years of reading super-hero comics, you just don't have the knowledge to fully appreciate *Watchmen* in its context. Any comics fan has that familiarity with the broad sketch of comic book history, however much of it they actually witnessed, whether they started reading when issues were a dime or a quarter or 50 cents.

The super-hero comic book as we know it started in 1938 with a bang: the first issue of *Action Comics,* starring Superman. There had been masked and costumed adventurers in literature and in pulp magazine adventures before – the Scarlet Pimpernel, Zorro, and the Shadow among them. The purple-clad jungle lawman the Phantom made his newspaper comic-strip appearance a year or two prior. But the convergence of the idea of a man in tights with extraordinary abilities fighting evil and the form of the primitive, four-color pamphlets that had begun appearing on newsstands (first with reprints of comic strips and then with new material) made magic happen – certainly financial magic, if only occasionally artistic magic. All of a sudden, there were masked, caped, winged, hooded, and helmeted characters everywhere; every beast, bird, or bug became an inspiration. Anyone with access to printable paper and newsstand distribution channels wanted to be a publisher; anyone who could use a typewriter churned out tales of damsels in distress, deathtraps, and diabolical villains; and anyone who could draw a passable figure – plus many who couldn't – stuck their arms in to illustrate these crude and fantastic stories for a couple of bucks while they waited for the real jobs in advertising or magazine art. They drew and wrote about and published super-heroes.

There had been and would continue to be comic books of other genres – humor, horror, romance, western, and war among them – but something about super-heroes and comic books put the whole enterprise into overdrive. Super-heroes and comics seemed made for each other. Only the comic-book page could contain these completely unrealistic scenarios and characters, presenting them in such a way that children could suspend their disbelief.

The start of World War II only opened the throttle wider. Given a strong moral platform on which to stand and a patriotic duty to perform, super-heroes reached even more dizzying heights of popularity. Flag-draped and star-spangled heroes joined the throng of costumed crime-fighters – and the war effort. This phase (spanning the birth of comics, the pre-war period, and the war years) has become known as the Golden Age.

What follows most golden ages is a dark period, and the post-war years were just that for comics. The end of combat brought a vacuum of purpose to the super-hero; the routine gangster boss or mad scientist seemed too weak an adversary for the men and women who had defeated fascism. The comics began to coast, bereft of the external force that had driven their rapid growth. Super-heroes began to wane in popularity, while lurid horror and crime comics stepped up to fill the void.

In 1948, both *Collier's Weekly* and the *American Journal of Psychotherapy* published articles by psychiatrist Frederic Wertham denouncing what he perceived as the psychopathy embodied in comic books, super-heroic or otherwise. Wertham kept up the drumbeat of warning over the next several years, until the publication of his book *Seduction of the Innocent* in 1954, leading to his appearance before the Senate Subcommittee on Juvenile Delinquency, chaired by Senator Estes Kefauver. Wertham testified that the explicit violence and hidden sexual themes of comic books led to antisocial behavior among their readers.

The massive wave of negative publicity put enough pressure on the comics industry that it neutered itself, for all intents and purposes, with the establishment of the Comics Code Authority – a self-censorship board somewhat similar to the MPAA, with its movie ratings, but with more specific rules, fewer options, and stringent oversight. Horror comics recoiled and died or moved to the magazine racks. The Western genre held on, as did romance, teen humor, war, and funny animal comics. Super-heroes, for the most part, devolved from pulp-style adventurers and patriotic-themed avengers to avuncular if strangely-dressed pals, as unthreatening and uncontroversial as possible, or they simply disappeared.

So complete was the devaluation of the super-hero that when DC Comics successfully introduced a new hero in the summer of 1956, the event would come to be regarded as the start of an era now called the Silver Age of Comics. Appearing first as a one-issue tryout in *Showcase* #4, the Flash took his name and super-speed powers from an earlier character who hadn't been seen on the newsstands in nearly a decade. The writers and artists who created this new version had also worked on the earlier Flash, and the new Flash was even shown as a fan of those wartime comics, taking his heroic name in tribute to his "fictional" predecessor.

With this, the floodgates were reopened. Once again, colorful heroes came swinging and swooping onto the scene. Companies like DC and Marvel started repopulating the super-hero scene. DC tended to offer stories that were more complex in structure, that were more plot-driven and science-based (some of their most successful writers also penned tales for the science fiction mags) but that remained juvenile in their moral outlook and lack of ambiguity. Marvel countered with more mature (read "adolescent") tales that were more character-driven and soap-opera flavored. Smaller houses like Charlton and MLJ Comics (the forerunner of Archie Comics) could once again support super-hero books of their own – some of which would be read by a young Alan Moore. Regardless of the publisher, all the heroes fought more alien invasions, would-be world-conquerors, evil monsters, and shadowy spy organizations than you could shake a cape at it. At times, it was gloriously silly; at times, it was mind-bogglingly bizarre. But it brought the super-hero back from the brink.

Straining at the shackles of the self-censoring Comics Code Authority, comics in the late Sixties started to become "relevant" – the social issues of the day once again papering the panels. Racial tensions, the antiwar movement, and drug use became unwieldy themes and unlikely plot points for gaudily-colored flying people who often seemed ill-at-ease confronting problems they couldn't punch. And as more and more former fans entered the comics business, this desire to expand the super-hero genre beyond its origins led to more attempts to layer "adult" storytelling onto a still-immature idiom. And so the Bronze Age of Comics, that awkward galoot of the Seventies, was born.

Comics wandered in this state for over a decade: neither fish nor fowl, a juvenile medium with pretensions to maturity, trying valiantly to be more than it had always been, and – with occasional flashes of lightning – usually failing. Until, as conventional wisdom would have it, *Watchmen* came along in 1985 to shift everything into a higher gear and move the whole medium forward – or at least a bit over to one side.

But if you weren't there, you have no idea what development comics had already gone through. If you haven't felt the pain of sticking with a medium and a genre both full of promise, each more disrespected than the other, there is so much in *Watchmen* you won't see. You won't look at the scenes set before the war and know that they evoke the Golden Age, aching with that passion for the crude and simple origins of the form characterized by comics critic Douglas Wolk as *nostalgie de la boue* – nostalgia for the gutter, the urge to slum. You won't see the connection between the strip-within-a-strip *Tales of the Black Freighter* and the real-world EC Comics, premier publisher of horror in the Fifties, whose publisher William Gaines was an embattled witness at the Kefauver hearings on Juvenile Deliquency. You'll get no resonance that the original Silk Spectre embodies (pun intended) the fashion for Good Girl Art or "Headlight" comics, or that the Crimebusters represent the not-quite-renaissance that was the Silver Age. You won't be able to understand how *Watchmen* is in many ways a self-referential history of the evolution of comics as well as the product of that evolution – a comic meant to be taken seriously. And without an intimate connection to the long, hard growing-up of comics, you'll have no way of knowing where *Watchman* fits in that history and just what an impact it made who had lived through its difficult early years.

This might be overstating the case. Even granting that familiarity with the historical context is necessary, you could still have a functional knowledge of the history of the super-hero without having been a fan. Television documentaries and recent magazine and newspaper articles that don't begin "Zap! Bam! Pow!" could offer you a sense of the big picture sufficient to put *Watchmen* in its context. But there's still another level of shared knowledge and accumulated lore needed to really appreciate *Watchmen*, another body of experience and expertise to inform your reading and reveal the subtlety and complexity of the work.

Take the now-iconic opening image of the Comedian being thrown through his apartment window as an example. Much can be gleaned by analysis of what is there – the use of color, the composition, and the ironic dialogue / caption box – but what struck experienced comics readers on first encountering this scene was what was not there: sound effects. For years, comics attempted to recreate the sound design of film and television through lettered sound indicators – a practice taken to its camp extreme in the *Batman* TV show when the words *Biff!* and *Pow!* were superimposed on screen.

Well-designed sound effects add to the narrative of the comic book page, helping to convey action, impact, and even nuance. Some artists handle their own sound effects and consider them part of the art; other books rely on letterers whose knowledge of typography allows them to create effects that are often art in their own right. In *Watchmen*, readers were faced with a comic that eschewed this basic, even emblematic, dimension of its own capabilities.

Besides the sound effects, something else is missing from this panel and from the rest of the book, something most casual readers likely don't even have a name for: those symbolic, non-diegetic graphic elements that cartoonist Mort Walker called *emanata*. Lines that indicate an object or person is moving at speed. Curved lines that indicate the swing of an arm. Dotted lines that indicate a character's line of sight. A starburst pattern that means something has been struck with force. None of these visual conventions appears in *Watchmen*.

Without sound effects and emanata, the images alone have to convey all the movement and action. Is someone standing, walking, or running? Only their positioning, the reactions of other characters in the scene, and our own knowledge of body mechanics clue us in. Is a bottle floating or falling? We have to look closely at the fluid inside and trust our innate sense of physics – there were no other markers to let us know. We were off the map, and this disorientation subtly added to the sense of differentness that pervaded the book.

Moore and Gibbons gave up yet another heretofore essential tool in the comics toolbox: while speech balloons are still used to portray the dialogue between characters, the closely-related *thought* balloon is nowhere to be found. As Rorschach surveys the apartment building, we don't magically "hear" his thoughts in a cloudy bubble with a dotted tail. (*"Hrm, I guess I'll have to use a grappling hook to scale that wall!"*) When Dan wakes from his disturbing dream for a midnight reverie, we can only deduce his emotions from his actions and not read his mind; his precise train of thought remains a mystery. This limitation somehow helped to ratchet up the "realism" of the book. Readers could still ignore the existence of the speech balloons, as we had learned to do, but the absence of thought balloons somehow made the whole story seem more serious.

By the same token, captions provide the "voice over" of speaking characters not seen within a panel, excerpts from Rorschach's journal, or even the captions from the *Tales of the Black Freighter* comic, but never authorial narration. Not even so much as a *"Meanwhile, back at Karnak..."* transition between scenes.

Watchmen was not the first comic-book story to dispense with these long-held conventions of comics storytelling, but it was certainly the most high-profile effort in that direction – suddenly forcing all subsequent creators to grapple with the choice of whether or not to employ these devices, when before *Watchmen* this wouldn't even have been considered an option.

The color was serious too. Comic books had long been associated with garish coloring; the limitations of traditional hand-coloring and the inefficiencies of the four-color separation process did not allow for much subtlety or sophistication. By the time *Watchmen* came along, advances in printing let colorist John Higgins use a more graduated, controlled – and darker – palette. This control allowed them to integrate the color as a narrative element, expanding the channels through which the story was communicated.

Another shift was manifested in Gibbons' page layout: most pages were composed on a straight-forward nine-panel grid, with occasional variation to accommodate a larger panel or two within the overall pattern. This system, actually a callback to typical Golden Age techniques, stood in direct contrast to the use of full-page scenes called "splash" pages – oversize panels, off-kilter and sometimes bizarre page layouts that had been growing more common during the Silver and Bronze Ages. This tight layout allowed for a significantly higher amount of plot development in the same page count and increased the impact of the few splash pages the story did feature.

Imagine you've never seen a ballet. A ballet enthusiast convinces you to attend a performance. You go along, reluctantly, and watch a bunch of people dancing. Maybe you even enjoy it. At the end, the enthusiast is flabbergasted. He can't believe what he's seen: the dancers broke most of the rules of ballet and made up a few of their own along the way. And it all worked! It was magnificent! Don't you agree? And you say, "Well, I thought it was pretty."

What else could you say? Without any familiarity with how ballet works, how can you explain why it was pretty? Without any knowledge of what it was supposed to look like, how can you tell it was anything different or special? Without experience of the everyday, how can you see the exceptional?

That's the position of reading *Watchmen* without a history as a comic book reader. Not having internalized the conventions and conceits of the medium, not having the sensitivity to the form and the vocabulary to describe it, you won't even know how exceptional a work it is.

So let's look at this set of criteria we've attempted to establish. A connection between the reader and the characters who were the prototypes for the protagonists? Surely that isn't entirely necessary to enjoy the book. A familiarity with other texts that informed the development of *Watchmen*? We can overlook that; it adds a layer of resonance but isn't directly related to the narrative. Some knowledge of comics and super-hero history? With the growing acceptance and legitimization of comics and graphic novels, we're all pretty close. A deep-seated, heartfelt intimacy with the language of comics? That seems essential... and without it, an entire layer of understanding will fail to emerge and *Watchmen* may be just another good book.

Of course, this is all exaggeration. *Watchmen* is a work of art, a masterpiece if you will, and such *magna opera* are timeless. We don't need to know details of seventeenth-century Dutch civic militia or be able to articulate the concept of *chiaroscuro* to view and appreciate Rembrandt's *Night Watch*, do we? So we don't really have to be comics scholars or historians to read and appreciate *Watchmen*. The multifaceted narrative, the complex storytelling, the detailed and beautiful artwork, the insightful social commentary, the important philosophical issues raised in this classic – all of these dimensions make the book not only accessible but valuable for a wide audience. Moore and Gibbons's masterwork can serve for anyone as a great example of the graphic novel.

But really, if you're not already a comics fan, don't read *Watchmen* first.

How the Ghost of You Clings: *Watchmen* and Music

by Mary Borsellino

Music runs through every stage of *Watchmen*'s life: it inspired Alan Moore and Dave Gibbons; it shaped the way they told their story in the graphic novel; it infuses the 2009 Zack Snyder film with historical and cultural relevance; and it's the creative medium of a number of *Watchmen*'s more famous fans. It loops and repeats, offering themes and variations throughout the story's lifespan. Understanding it means adding a new layer of our understanding of the work as a whole.

Structurally, *Watchmen* is shaped not only by individual songs or artists but by the possibilities present in music as an art form. Moore has cited experimental writer William S Burroughs as a main influence, and *Nova Express*, one of *Watchmen*'s in-world print publications, is named after a Burroughs novel. Moore has explained that Burroughs's mark on *Watchmen* can be found in Moore's attempts to "put some of [Burroughs's] ideas into practice; the idea of repeated symbols that would become laden with meaning. You could almost play them like music. You'd have these things like musical themes that would occur throughout the work."

The *Nova Express* interview with Adrian Veidt near the end of *Watchmen* contains many of the story's most telling and explicit references to music.

Veidt's servant is quoted as saying, "he's not one of your pop music stars" as a way of vouching for Veidt's lily-white moral character – he's not a drug user, he doesn't sleep with groupies, he doesn't take advantage of his wealth. But only a few paragraphs later, journalist Doug Roth is describing Veidt's appeal in rock-star terms: "Every girlfriend I've had in the past four years has wanted to nail this guy, more than Jagger, more than Springsteen or D'Eath or any of those also-rans." The film version further emphasizes the link between Veidt and the larger-than-life world of pop icons, showing him hanging out at Studio 54 with Bowie, Jagger, and the Village People.

Veidt may himself not be a "pop music star" but he has a kind of fame which can only be articulated through the language of that type of celebrity. The theatricality and charisma of super-heroes finds its closest real-world analog in the rock star, a fact which equates the superhuman feats – and the violence – performed by *Watchmen*'s heroes with the metaphorical foundation-shaking that pop music can perform on society. Consider Hollis Mason's remarks about the cultural revolution of the mid-20th century and its effect on the heroes of the time:

> Partly it was the beatniks, the jazz musicians and the poets openly condemning American values whenever they opened their mouths. Partly it was Elvis Presley and the whole Rock and Roll boom. Had we fought a war for our country so that our daughters could scream and swoon over young men who looked like *this*, who sounded like *that*?

Keep in mind that Mason himself looks like a policeman dressed up as an owl in a pair of armored shorts. Super-heroes are rock stars and rock stars are super-heroes, no matter how much Veidt's servant may wish otherwise.

(Even the "Elvis lives" conspiracy theories of the real world are echoed in speculation by author James Gifford that early heroes Hooded Justice and Captain Metropolis may have faked their presumed deaths and can be seen alive and well in the first chapter of *Watchmen*... a conjecture neither confirmed nor denied by Dave Gibbons when asked about it.)

Near the end of his *Nova Express* interview, Veidt describes his musical tastes:

> I like electronic music. That's a very superhero-ey thing to like, I suppose, isn't it? I like avant-garde music in general. Cage, Stockhausen, Penderecki, Andrew Lang, Pierre Henry. Terry Riley is very good. Oh, and I've heard some interesting new music from Jamaica... a sort of hybrid between electronic music and reggae. It's a fascinating study in the new musical forms generated when a largely pre-technological culture is given

> access to modern recording techniques about the technological preconceptions that we've allowed to accumulate, limiting out vision. It's called dub music. You'd like it, I'm sure.

These choices contain hidden significance worth examining.

John Cage was regarded by many people as the most influential American composer of the 20th century. His most famous work is the 1952 composition *4'33"*, which contains no notes. It was intended to be heard as the sounds of the environment around the listener rather than simply silence – an artistic intent which finds a dark echo in Rorschach's assertion that existence is meaningless, save for that meaning we impose upon it. Cage believed that music was "not an attempt to bring order out of chaos nor to suggest improvements in creation, but simply a way of waking up to the very life we're living," which is a considerably different attitude to that employed by Veidt himself.

Karlheinz Stockhausen, like John Cage, was seen by many as a deeply important 20th-century composer. Some of his most ground-breaking work was in the field of aleatoricism – art created through controlled randomness. The William S. Burroughs novel *Nova Express* is another example of aleatoricism: the book was created out of pre-existing texts that were cut into sections and reassembled in random order, in an effort to uncover previously hidden meanings in the text.

Polish composer and conductor Krzysztof Penderecki came to world attention for his 1960 composition *Threnody to the Victims of Hiroshima*. The piece was featured in the 1982 British film *QED: A Guide To Armageddon*, which simulated the outcomes of a nuclear bomb being exploded over London.

Andrew Lang was a Scottish writer: novels, poems, literary criticism, and – apparently of most interest to Veidt – metrical experiments. His strongest legacy has been as a collector of folk and fairy tales.

Pierre Henry, a French composer, was one of the founding artists behind major electronic music techniques, particularly the incorporation of sound other than that made by musical instruments or voices. Without this breakthrough in thinking, mainstays of electronica such as looping, slowing-down or speeding-up of a recording, and the creation of the synthesizer would never have occurred. Henry's "outside the box" application of existing technologies to create outcomes beyond traditional thinking make him an obvious choice as one of Veidt's favorites, though Veidt's choices have a considerably darker impact on human history.

Terry Riley is an American minimalist composer perhaps best known today for his influential works *In C* and *A Rainbow in Curved Air*. In the 1960s, he would perform improvised music from dusk until dawn, employing an organ harmonium and a tape-delayed saxophone. When he grew too tired to play, he would replay looped fragments recorded earlier in the evening – a technique mimicked by the (wholly new) inclusion of historical materials interspersed throughout *Watchmen*.

"Dub" is short for "double"; a song's dub version typically emphasizes the original's beat elements, lowers the bass pitch, and reduces or removes the vocal and instrumental elements. Dub revises existing songs just as the *Watchmen* universe is Moore and Gibbons' super-hero-based revision of the real world. Dub music, despite being carefully constructed, has a very organic feel. As Veidt says, Dub music originated in Jamaica, specifically in Duke Reid's Treasure Isle studio in 1968. Sound system operator Ruddy Redwood wanted to create a "dub-plate" – a quality-control disc created before a studio commits to a master recording – but the engineer left the vocal track off by accident. Redwood kept the end result, playing it at his next dance while an MC rapped over it. The name of the studio, tying in as it does to *Watchmen*'s motifs of piracy and buried treasure, may well have been known to Moore.

Veidt's remarks about using modern techniques while shedding modern preconceptions can also be read as a remark on the narrow focus employed by mainstream comics. Despite the near-limitless potential of sequential art, the overwhelming majority of titles produced by American comics publishers in 1986 were super-hero stories. This becomes the basis for the extreme popularity of pirate-themed comics in the world of *Watchmen*: a world where super-heroes really exist would be unlikely to be interested in super-hero comics, so another equally niche genre becomes monolithic. The result, while not quite parody, nevertheless reveals the absurdity of the mainstream comics industry. Through Veidt's comments regarding dub music, Moore arguably ponders what might happen if our vision suddenly ceased to be limited by preconceptions of what comics should be.

The comic story running within *Watchmen* itself, "Tales of the Black Freighter" takes its name from the lyrics of the song "Pirate Jenny" from the play *The Threepenny Opera*, written by Berthold Brecht and composer Kurt Weill. The song's original German name is "Seeräuberjenny," and it details the revenge fantasies of a lowly hotel cleaner named Jenny Diver who imagines the day when a ship – "the Black Freighter" – will come into harbor and completely destroy the town which oppresses her. Then the ship will head back out to sea, and when it leaves she will be on it, becoming the Pirate Jenny.

The "Black Freighter" comic-within-a-comic can be read as an allegory for several of the central characters in the main story of *Watchmen*, but Moore himself has said it was designed to parallel the arc of Adrian Veidt. Both Veidt and the central character of the "Black Freighter" are driven to increasingly abhorrent acts in an effort to save civilization, culminating in bloody murder in order to perhaps prevent wider carnage.

(The song obviously holds a special place in Moore's affections. The third volume of Moore and Kevin O'Neill's *League of Extraordinary Gentlemen*, entitled *Century*, opens with an installment recounting an apochryphal tale of Pirate Jenny herself. In this case, her story leads to the revelation that the Black Freighter is a seagoing vessel already well-known from another work of fiction – a twist in keeping with the overall theme of Moore and O'Neill's *League,* in which all fictional characters are real.)

Berthold Brecht's work is famous for using the art form of the theatrical production in ways that challenged the form's traditional limits, much as *Watchmen* challenged and redefined the comics form. Ironically, two of the methods employed by Brecht to break down the accepted limits of theatre were the projection of captions over the stage and having characters carry picket-signs. Both elements are present in *Watchmen*, but here they slip seamlessly into the narrative rather than disrupting it.

By the time Moore wrote *Watchmen*, "Pirate Jenny" had a set of deeply significant metaphorical meanings attached to it, thanks to the version of the song performed by singer Nina Simone. "Pirate Jenny" was included on the 1964 album *Nina Simone in Concert*, along with a selection of civil rights songs such as "Mississippi Goddam" and "Old Jim Crow." Simone transformed "Pirate Jenny" into a civil rights song as well, making "the Black Freighter" a metaphor for an African-American force powerful enough to destroy the racism and intolerance of the American South, while also making the title character's feelings of rage and desire for vengeance immediate and visceral. Simone did not perform the song often, saying it took so much energy out of her that it required seven years for her to recover after each performance.

"Pirate Jenny" was also a strong influence on the highly political folk songs of Bob Dylan. Biographer Clinton Heylin says, of Dylan's 1964 album *The Times*

They Are a-Changing, that "as Pirate Jenny dreams of the destruction of all her enemies by a mysterious ship, so Dylan envisages the neophobes being swept aside in 'the hour when the ship comes in.'" The album's title song would eventually be heard playing under the opening sequence of the *Watchmen* movie. The album also includes the song "The Lonesome Death of Hattie Carroll," which tells the story of a black female hotel worker beaten to death by a white man, based on a real-world event that represented for Dylan how lightly the American justice system valued the life of a black woman. Pirate Jenny may dream of revenge, but Hattie Carroll was the likely reality for someone in that position.

Less than two years later, Dylan wrote and recorded the song "Desolation Row," which was to become one of the starting points for the creation of *Watchmen*. The opening lyrics of "Desolation Row" reference the murder by lynching in 1920 of three black circus workers in Duluth, Minnesota, which happened within a few blocks of where Dylan's father lived at the time. A photograph of the dead, still-hanging bodies of the three men was later made into a postcard and offered for sale.

An unfortunate complication arises from the use of "Desolation Row" and the Black Freighter of "Pirate Jenny" in *Watchmen*: all the black characters seen in *Watchmen* die horribly during the execution of Veidt's plan. The Black Freighter has come to sack the town, but it is not a moment of metaphorical civil rights revolution of the kind presented by Simone. The instigator of the mass murder is Veidt – a blonde Caucasian man – and aside from Veidt, the two main characters we follow as survivors after the mass murder are Laurie Juspeczyk and Dan Dreiberg. Both are white, and in their new identities in the brave new world of Veidt, both are blonde.

The focus becomes even narrower: the future of this world, the reader learns, is "entirely in your hands," but the hands in question belong to a staff member of a racist, right-wing organization which has earlier been shown supporting the actions of the Ku Klux Klan. Revolution has come, but it's a revolution absolutely at odds with what "Pirate Jenny" represents in pop culture.

When interviewed in *Entertainment Weekly* about the film adaptation of *Watchmen*, directed by Zack Snyder, Moore referenced Snyder's earlier film *300* – itself based on a graphic novel by Frank Miller – in explaining why he did not intend to see the film of *Watchmen*:

> I didn't particularly like the book *300*. I had a lot of problems with it, and everything I heard or saw about the film tended to increase [those problems] rather than reduce them: [that] it was racist, it was homophobic, and above all it was sublimely stupid.

While Moore evidently does not consider himself racist or homophobic, this does not mean that works created by him cannot be unintentionally guilty of these sins.

Another song quoted as a chapter end in *Watchmen* is John Cale's "Sanities." Intended by Cale to be called "Sanctus," it was mislabelled and issued as "Santies" when an engineer couldn't read Cale's handwriting. Later printings corrected this to "Sanities." Like most of the music enjoyed by Veidt, this period in Cale's career was marked by his spare, spacious instrumentation.

The music of *Watchmen*'s world, like the world itself, has some touchstones of similarity with our own world and some divergences. Billie Holiday and Devo are both present in the popular culture of the book's world; they serve as a metaphor for the generational gulf between Dan Dreiberg and Laurie Juspeczyk. Dan – old enough to have owned a pornographic Tijuana Bible featuring Laurie's mother, at a time when Laurie herself was still only four years old – is a Holiday fan; Laurie doesn't recognize her voice. Devo, on the other hand, is modern enough that when Laurie makes reference to them, Dan doesn't understand. This is one of the book's few nods to the fact that both of Laurie's lovers, Dan Dreiberg and Jon Osterman, are sufficiently older than her that they can be plausible father substitutes as well as romantic partners. Indeed, both the second Nite Owl and Dr. Manhattan, in their super-hero days, worked alongside Laurie's real father.

Music that exists in the world of Watchmen but not in our own world serves primarily as a vehicle for foreboding imagery. There is an upcoming "stupid dyke disco" benefit performance for the organization Gay Women Against Rape (GWAR), with the poster advertising this event later torn in Veidt's attack on New York, now simply reading "WAR." The centerpiece of Veidt's carnage is Madison Square Garden, where the bands Pale Horse and Krystalnacht were in mid-concert, their crowds of fans now a horrifying tableau of bodies.

"Krystalnacht" alludes to "Kristallnacht," the night in November 1938 in which Nazis rounded up 25 to 30 thousand German Jews and took them to concentration camps, destroyed hundreds of synagogues, and ransacked thousands of businesses. Many historians now cite Kristallnacht as one of the

One of the most direct musical references in *Watchmen* but far from the only one.
From *Watchmen* #7 (March 1987). Copyright © DC Comics.

key points in the progression of Nazi doctrine toward its later mass genocide. Literally, "Kristallnacht" means "the night of shattered glass," a name echoed hauntingly by Gibbons's depiction of New York following Veidt's attack, in which the streets are littered with the remnants of broken windows.

"Pale Horse" is the literal translation from Greek of the Fourth Horseman of the Apocalypse, as described in Revelation 6:8, commonly referred to as "Death" in English-language media. The lead singer of Pale Horse is named "Red D'Eath," which may be an allusion to the Edgar Allan Poe story "The Masque of the Red Death." The Red Death of Poe's story is an agonizing and gory plague killing those infected almost instantly. Like Moore's novel, Poe's short story utilizes repeated images related to time and blood.

The vicious punk gang members responsible for the murder of Hollis Mason belong to a subculture called Knot Tops, who take their fashion cues from Red D'Eath. One of the Knot Tops, Derf, is depicted in the film version of *Watchmen* wearing an upside-down Anarchy symbol on his clothing. Upside-down, the Anarchy 'A' becomes a shape halfway between the original symbol and the V employed by the lead character in Moore's *V for Vendetta*, while also offering a dark counterpoint to the $ symbol on the hero Dollar Bill's costume, and the iconographic S of Superman.

At a 2009 screening of the Zack Snyder film, Dave Gibbons noted that the lyric beginning "Now at midnight all the agents," from Bob Dylan's "Desolation Row," had been one of the starting points of the *Watchmen* comic. This was merely the beginning of Dylan's influence on the story. His "All Along the Watchtower" is not only the source for a chapter title but also provides imagery echoed in the comic: one chapter ends with the quote "outside in the cold distance, a wildcat did growl. Two riders were approaching, and the wind began to howl." In the panels of the story itself, Bubastis the lynx, inside Adrian's compound, growls at images of Rorschach and Nite Owl approaching through the snowstorm on their hover-scooters.

The phrase "the times they are a-changing" is used as the text in an ad for Nostalgia perfume in 1975, despite the ad's intended connotations being at direct odds with Dylan's song of the same name. Looking back 21 years after creating the song, Dylan explained in 1985, "I wanted to write a big song, with short concise verses that piled up on each other in a hypnotic way. The civil rights movement and the folk music movement were pretty close for a while and allied together at that time." In contrast, Veidt's perfume brand Nostalgia is designed to appeal to fear of change and the desire to cling to the familiar and known. Part of Veidt's plan for his brave new world involves phasing out Nostalgia in favor of the presumably forward-looking scent Millennium. "The Times They Are a-Changing" is also used in the Snyder film, where it serves as the soundtrack to the title sequence, as a series of images depicting the history of costumed super-heroes.

Another song that appears in both the comic and the film but in very different contexts is "The Ride of the Valkyries" from the opera *Die Walküre* by Richard Wagner. In the graphic novel, original Nite Owl Hollis Mason makes reference to the song in an anecdote from his young, pre-super-heroic days, explaining that "every time I hear it I get depressed and start wondering about the lot of humanity and the unfairness of life and all those other things." In the film, the song is the soundtrack to Dr. Manhattan and the Comedian's involvement in the Vietnam War, incorporating an echo of Francis Ford Coppola's 1979 film *Apocalypse Now*. This invocation allows themes from *Apocalypse Now* to cast shadows onto *Watchmen* – specifically, ideas of American imperialism over the world and the darkness in human nature. So too does the song's use play with the generic pop-culture standing of "Ride of the Valkyries" as a song now associated with on-screen depictions of the military, stemming from its use in *Apocalypse Now*.

Just as music was a deeply significant influence on the creation of *Watchmen*, so too has *Watchmen* been an influence on music. The graphic novel's impact on several highly popular bands serves as a demonstration of the large ripple effect a work of art of *Watchmen*'s stature can have on subsequent creative acts.

The musician with the closest associations to *Watchmen* is, of course, Alan Moore himself. Heavily involved in the 1980s punk scene, Moore wrote music journalism under the pseudonym Curt Vile, a punning reference to *Threepenny Opera* composer Kurt Weill. Moore's 1980s band the Sinister Ducks released a recording of "This Vicious Cabaret," a song originating in Moore's *V for Vendetta*. Moore also recorded two tracks as "Eddie Enrico and His Hawaiian Hotshots" for inclusion with copies of *The League of Extraordinary Gentlemen: Black Dossier*. As well as writing music to go with his comics, several of Moore's songs have been turned into comics themselves, published by Caliber Comics and Avatar. Considering how heavily music is incorporated into *Watchmen* itself, it is perhaps unsurprising that Moore never created a musical tie-in for that particular book.

In 1989, English band Pop Will Eat Itself released the song "Can U Dig It" which names Alan Moore and *V for Vendetta* directly in its lyrics. The music video features members of the band in front of a wall of television sets highly reminiscent of Veidt's setup, as well as heavy use of a variety of panels from the *Watchmen* graphic novel. The song was taken from the album *This is the Day... This is the Hour... This is This!* The same album includes a track called "Def Con One," also inspired by *Watchmen* and even mentioning the comic by name. The "Can U Dig It" video tied the world of music and the world of *Watchmen* together into a single unit; music fans who hadn't encountered the comic before were introduced to it when the single entered the Top 40 in the U.K.... while the comics industry and fandom had concrete evidence that the pop-culture significance of Alan Moore and *Watchmen* had reached an iconic level.

Winnipeg guitarist Joey Serlin named his late-Eighties alternative rock band the Watchmen as a nod to the graphic novel, of which he was a fan. The band went on to be one of Canada's most commercially successful alternative groups of the late 1990s, sharing rotation time with Pop Will Eat Itself and further cementing Moore's place in the pop music lexicon.

New Yorker Jeffrey Lewis's acoustic punk music is often tagged as "antifolk" for the way it deconstructs the earnest sensibilities of the 1960s folk movement. His current discography includes more than 20 releases, and he has written essays on songwriting for *The New York Times* online. Lewis's lyrically sophisticated songs are simultaneously bleak and optimistic, informed by his appreciation of Leonard Cohen and of New York City itself. As well as sharing this contextually similar frame of influences with *Watchmen*, Lewis's career has been as much about the comic as it has been about his own musical work. His 1997 senior thesis at the State University of New York was on *Watchmen*, and he has given cultural studies lectures in Belgium and America analyzing the book. Lewis's analysis of *Watchmen* (published as "The Dual Nature of Apocalypse in *Watchmen*" in the book *The Graphic Novel*, edited by Jan Baetens) centers around themes of vision being obscured and becoming cleared, of structural homages to William Blake's *Songs of Innocence* and *Songs of Experience*, and the clashes between Veidt's man-made triangle motifs and the circles and loops of natural order, which ultimately triumph over the triangular forms. Lewis is also an accomplished underground comics creator in his own right.

Popular Chicago pop-punk band Fall Out Boy collaborated with Elvis Costello on their 2008 song "What a Catch, Donnie." Costello's song "The Comedians" is among those whose lyrics are quoted in *Watchmen*, bringing Fall Out Boy within the same frame of reference as the story. The connections between the band and the graphic novel run much deeper, however, with drummer Andy Hurley citing it as his favorite book, explaining in his online journal that *Watchmen* is

> probably the greatest piece of fiction ever written. It is an absolute masterpiece, in every sense. Its depth, complexity, mastery of the art form[,] and amazing story all come together to create perfection in one graphic novel. It is historical. Read this before you see the movie, which could be good, or could be the biggest piece of shit. Either way, it has nothing to do with the graphic novel, which stands in a league of its own.

However, the band with arguably the deepest connection to *Watchmen* is the New Jersey punk quintet My Chemical Romance. The band's lead singer Gerard Way explained in an opinion piece for the British newspaper *The Guardian*: "*Watchmen* is not only the greatest comic ever written, it's a really important work of fiction. More so than any record, it was the first thing that really made me say to myself, 'This is what I want to do.' Way went on to elaborate:

> The thing about *Watchmen* that people should know is that when it came out there was absolutely nothing like it. Up until then comics were about the same thing: a guy in tights fighting another guy in tights and saving the girl – that was it. The only touch of reality might be Peter Parker getting a cold. When I was in high school and listening to a lot of punk rock and watching *Taxi Driver*, Rorschach was a character I could identify with. [...] He's angry and he sees the world in the way that I saw the world at the time. As I got older[,] I identified with Nite Owl more. Then, to some extent, I became a lot more interested in the Comedian. He's the most real character in the story because he has so many faults, more than anyone in the book.

On My Chemical Romance's second album, 2004's *Three Cheers for Sweet Revenge*, one of the songs is titled "The Ghost of You," acknowledged by Way as taken from *Watchmen*'s advertising slogan for Nostalgia, "Oh, how the ghost of you clings." (The phrase originated in another song, the popular 1936 standard "These Foolish Things," revealing yet another point where Moore drew richness from the world of music in order to strengthen his story.)

My Chemical Romance is the only group or artist on the *Watchmen* film soundtrack whose recording does not originate from 1985 or earlier. Way explained the group's cover version of Dylan's "Desolation Row" in his *Guardian* article: "Our version came from a desire to do something 'of its era,' which in the case of Watchmen is an alternate 1980s. I wanted the music to feel like how youth culture might feel at the time, so we approached it like an [']80s new wave song." Zack Snyder directed the cover song's music video, released as the movie soundtrack's feature single. In the video, My Chemical Romance play a midtown Manhattan theater which lists Pale Horse as an upcoming act; the Empire State Building looms mere blocks away as the Gunga Diner balloon drifts overhead. The band's performance is disrupted when a fight breaks out among the audience populated by Knot Tops, and the riot police storm in. After the music video was released, Gerard Way again made reference to *Watchmen* in the band's blog, saying:

> Serious life-long dream to be a part of this film in some way, and we were lucky enough to have Zack direct it. He did a bang up job. [...] Some of my favorite people on the set were the guys that played the "Knot-Tops", which is a street-gang from the comic. So I snapped a picture of them hanging out... I would say this is in continuity...

In addition to being a rock musician, Way is also the author of the critically-acclaimed and Eisner Award-winning comic series *The Umbrella Academy*. In an interview with the site Comic Book Resources, Way explained the connection between his own work and *Watchmen*: "One of my favorite aspects of *Watchmen* was that Alan Moore cared enough about the characters to actually kill them, for real." In his *Guardian* article, Way also elaborated the ways he was inspired by the earlier comic:

> My comic series, *The Umbrella Academy*, is absolutely indebted to *Watchmen*. You don't want to rip somebody off, but you want to explore things they started to explore. Even if it's just characters having an awkward conversation while drinking coffee on a rooftop or in a diner. The fact that the characters in *Umbrella Academy* already had a history was definitely a nod to *Watchmen*, too. And the fact that they're all 30 and the fun of their youth is kind of over.

If the final words of *Watchmen* are read as a call to arms for future creators – announcing that the comics medium has been left entirely in their hands – then Way is one of the most striking new voices, picking up where Moore left off and making what came next his own.

Watchmen borrowed extensively from music but left things, at the end of the graphic novel, "entirely in [our] hands" – encouraging readers to create their own, equally vital works of art. And so the loop-like form of the natural order of things manifests itself in the life of *Watchmen* as a story and a cultural artifact. In the case of My Chemical Romance, this manifested both in Way's own comic stories, influenced by but not beholden to *Watchmen*'s legacy, and in the film's cover version of "Desolation Row." Fittingly, the song begins over the final shot of the film, depicting Rorschach's journal in a pile of letters, awaiting possible discovery. In this sense, as Way put it, his own work can indeed be argued to be "in continuity."

The Smartest Man in the Morgue: *Watchmen* and "Twelve Notes on the Mystery Story"

by Chad Nevett

Like so many other mystery stories before it, *Watchmen* begins with a body. The corpse belongs to Edward Blake, a.k.a. the Comedian, a costumed hero turned government operative. Before the story opens, someone has broken into Blake's apartment, beaten him savagely, and hurled him through the window to the pavement below. Our investigating detective is urban vigilante Rorschach, who believes the murderer is targeting "capes" – former costumed heroes. This theory seems confirmed when one hero is driven off the face of the Earth, another is the target of an assassination attempt, and Rorschach himself is framed for murder. Ultimately, Rorschach and his former partner Nite Owl discover that retired hero Adrian Veidt is behind the whole thing. Having killed Blake to prevent the exposure of Veidt's secret plan to save the world – a plan that also required Dr. Manhattan's removal from the scene – Veidt staged the attempt on his own life, deflecting suspicion from himself while apparently supporting Rorschach's theory until the latter could be sent away to prison. But Veidt has not anticipated the tenacity of Rorschach, nor the decency of Nite Owl, and their efforts uncover the truth.

That is the murder mystery plot of *Watchmen* in a nutshell. For all the praise and discussion devoted to *Watchmen*, little of it is directed at the mystery plot – the driving force behind the story. On the surface, it seems like a well-constructed mystery... but does it hold up to the standards of one of the 20th century's greatest mystery writers?

Raymond Chandler is most famous for his series of novels featuring private detective Philip Marlowe, including *The Big Sleep* (1939); *Farewell, My Lovely* (1940), and *The Long Goodbye* (1953), as well as short story collections such as *The Simple Art of Murder* (1950). As a screenwriter in Hollywood, Chandler worked on the scripts for *Double Indemnity* (1944), *The Blue Dahlia* (1946), and *Strangers on a Train* (1951). Along with his contemporary Dashiell Hammett, Chandler defined the "hardboiled" style of detective story, in which a hero of great integrity not only solved a murder mystery in a grim urban setting but faced dangers he had to escape through his wits, resourcefulness, and toughness. Chandler began his career writing for the pulps of the 1930s, which also gave birth to comic books; suspense and fast-paced action were highly valued there.

Chandler outlined his conception of what a mystery plot requires to work in an essay called "Twelve Notes on the Mystery Story." The essay contains the twelve main notes along with 13 additional addenda (taken from Chandler's final revised version of 18 April 1948) and offer a compilation of what Chandler thought the ideal mystery story should be. That any one story, including Chandler's own writings, satisfies all these requirements is nearly impossible – but they are interesting standards by which to examine mysteries. Though this is only one standard by which to judge the mystery plot in *Watchmen*, these notes from a master of the genre are quite comprehensive and cover almost every conceivable aspect of mystery stories, sometimes even contradicting one another.

Now, let's introduce Mr. Moore to Mr. Chandler.

For his first note, Chandler writes that the mystery "must be credibly motivated, both as to the original situation and the denouement; it must consist of the plausible actions of plausible people in plausible circumstances, it being remembered that plausibility is largely a matter of style," adding that "trick endings" or elaborate plots that rely heavily on coincidence are also examples of poor writing. There are really two parts to this note, the second of which Chandler enunciates more completely later. The first is a question of motivation, which Moore satisfies: Veidt wants to save the world and is afraid Blake will expose his plot. Veidt has reason to fear this, as a drunken Blake broke into the home of an old enemy and blathered like an insane man, dropping various hints and allusions to Veidt's plan. While Blake may not have taken it further, he represented a risk, and Veidt could not take the chance that Blake would keep quiet from then on. Veidt's plot was years in the making, giving him more than enough motivation in keeping it from being revealed. That his goal was preventing total nuclear war adds a benevolent aspect to his plan, giving it more urgency, at least in the eyes of the reader. If you carry Veidt's motivation through to the other elements of his plan, such as giving cancer to former associates of Dr. Manhattan in an effort to drive him from Earth and framing Rorschach for murder, his motivation holds up, as those two characters have the ability to discover his scheme and alter it.

Veidt's motivation and actions may be called into question in that his plan concludes with killing a sizable portion of New York's population. Does his goal of uniting the planet and preventing nuclear war require so large a loss of life, or could we reasonably expect the so-called "world's smartest man" to create a more sophisticated, less bloody solution to the problem? This is a grey area where the results are unclear. Since we are ultimately shown the plan succeeding as originally intended, there is no other option than to accept Veidt's motivation as credible.

The first note is expanded in the second note, where Chandler writes "It must be technically sound as to the methods of murder and detection." Really, this note has two parts to it as well: the murder itself and how the murder is solved by the detective. Chandler is very adamant that the murder should be as simple as possible in execution and not rely heavily on "fantastic poisons" or other unbelievable or unlikely means. Veidt murders Blake by breaking into his apartment, physically assaulting him, and throwing him through a window – a highly believable and simple manner by which to kill someone.

As for the detective, Chandler is specific in demanding that he must not only be capable but

> must at least know enough about police methods not to make an ass of himself. When a policeman is made out to be a fool, as he always was on the Sherlock Holmes stories, this not only depreciates the accomplishment

of the detective, but it also makes the reader doubt the author's knowledge of his own field.

Of course, this does not mean there cannot be animosity between the detective and the police – or that, by solving the case before the police, a detective is making the police look like fools. It simply means that the detective should not walk into a crime scene and notice something so painfully obvious the only conclusion is that the police are incompetent.

There is room for debate whether this is the case in *Watchmen* when Rorschach discovers Blake's secret closet containing his Comedian costume, weapons, and other items. He discovers this by noticing that the closet does not go as deep as it should, but this is a very subtle and not immediately obvious thing to notice. This discovery is the moment where the investigations by Rorschach and the police part ways. Blake being the Comedian immediately raises new possibilities, so this is the only spot where the argument could be made for Moore depicting Rorschach as superior to the police in a way that depicts the police as fools. Had Rorschach known ahead of time that Blake was the Comedian, this knowledge would give him an advantage. Instead, he tells Dan Dreiberg he "investigated a routine homicide victim named Edward Blake. Found the costume in Blake's wardrobe. Seems he was the Comedian." However, his discovery is an odd and subtle one; he uses a coat hanger to determine that the closet is shallow by only a few inches – a very easy thing to overlook. The police do not appear particularly foolish in missing that, and the same officers are later shown to be reasonably astute in discerning the civilian identity of Nite Owl.

For the rest of the story, Rorschach's methods seem sound enough, considering that his own personal bias leads him entirely on the wrong path. Having assumed that Blake was killed by someone targeting costumed heroes, his methods in pursuing that angle are effective – but mostly worthless, since it is the wrong direction to take the investigation. He contacts other former costumed heroes, both to warn them and to question them about the murder, since all are likely suspects considering the skills they possess. He stakes out Blake's funeral for anyone suspicious and notices Moloch, a former criminal, who reveals Blake's drunken visit – the catalyst in Veidt's decision to kill Blake, though Rorschach has no way of knowing this. These seemingly correct steps prompt Veidt to frame Rorschach for Moloch's murder and fake an assassination attempt against himself, fooling not only Rorschach but the

The investigator begins his investigation. From *Watchmen* #1 (September 1986).
Copyright © DC Comics.

readers as well into believing the "mask killer" theory. Only after Nite Owl and the Silk Spectre break Rorschach out of prison do they discover Veidt is behind the entire thing. Despite being the central detective of the story, Rorschach's own failings make him unable to solve the case, despite having demonstrated the skills necessary to do so. Because Rorschach has the skill and knowledge to solve the murder but is limited by his personal problems, Moore satisfies Chandler's requirements while also having the detective fail, an interesting and difficult feat to pull off.

Rorschach's mistaken assumption early on leads us to Chandler's third note:

> [The mystery story] must be honest with the reader. This is always said, but the implications are not realized. Important facts not only must not be concealed, they must not be distorted by false emphasis. Unimportant facts must not be projected in such a way as to make them portentous. (This creation of red herrings and false menace out of trick camera work and mood shots is the typical Hollywood mystery picture cheat.) Inferences from the facts are the detective's stock in trade; but he should disclose enough to keep the reader's mind working.

One might suspect *Watchmen* risks failing this requirement: false clues and red herrings develop as part of Rorschach's investigation since, for much of the book, readers think the story is about a simple plot to kill costumed heroes. But cleverly, Moore actually adheres to Chandler's requirements here: all of the necessary information to see the larger picture is provided, and the false emphasis on certain facts or misinterpretation of events is given by the characters themselves. Not only that, but Veidt creates false clues in order to cover his tracks, as a result of Rorschach's investigation. For example, having learned that Veidt faked his own attempted assassination, the reader may then return to that scene and recognize that Veidt places a poison capsule in the killer's mouth to create the impression of a suicide. None of this is an attempt by Moore to deceive readers or keep them in the dark through suspect means. If anything, the reader is fooled because the story satisfies this criterion, making sure Rorschach discloses every inference and idea related to his investigation. He simply happens to be wrong.

Chandler's fourth note hits on one of the most notable and discussed elements of *Watchmen*: its realistic characters and settings. Chandler thinks that a good mystery "must be about real people in the real world," arguing that "[i]t makes the difference between the story you reread and remember and the one you skim through and almost instantly forget." In this regard, there is little question that *Watchmen* satisfies this note. While it does involve many fantastic elements, *Watchmen* is realistic in character, setting, and atmosphere. One of Moore's intentions in the book was "to treat the world that the... heroes live in exactly as our world, but to actually try to work out and follow through on the implications of the presence of super-heroes," and in that respect, he succeeds. As for the re-readability of *Watchmen*, its continuing success and critical status is self-evident, answering Chandler's fifth note that a good mystery should have value beyond the mystery itself. In trying to create a fully-realized world, Moore and Gibbons extend far beyond the confines of the mystery, which in and of itself would be an interesting-enough read, thanks to Rorschach's unique character and personality. By devoting whole issues and parts of issues to the numerous other characters populating this world, from other costumed heroes to newsstand vendors and other average people, *Watchmen* goes far beyond the mystery plot.

"To achieve this it must have some form of suspense, even if only intellectual," Chandler writes in his sixth note. "This does not mean menace and especially it does not mean that the detective must be menaced by grave personal danger... But there must be conflict, physical, ethical or emotional, and there must be some element of danger in the broadest sense of the word." There is a constant feel of imminent threat, mostly because of the Cold War standoff between the U.S. and Russia. It is not just the main characters who are threatened but their entire world. As well, relationships begin and die, characters are killed or imprisoned or attacked. It is not a constant onslaught of terror, but there is a continual feeling of suspense throughout the story. In this note, Chandler also mentions that "over-plotted" stories can be bores – a critique often leveled at Moore, since his stories are so meticulously constructed, full of little tricks and fully-formed visual motifs. While *Watchmen* does at times feel a little over-plotted, it is also one of Moore's most energetic books, since it grew and changed as he and Gibbons completed it, as he later recounted: "Somewhere along the way, in between the material we were working with and the new narrative techniques we were attempting, something began to happen that we really hadn't anticipated." This pushing of boundaries provides the "color, lift, and a reasonable amount of dash" that Chandler requires in his seventh note as well.

Chandler's eighth, ninth, and tenth notes all concern the actual solution to the mystery and form a coherent picture of Chandler's ideal solution in its revelation to the reader. In these notes, Chandler suggests three essential qualities: it "must have enough essential simplicity to be explained easily when the time comes," it "must baffle a reasonably intelligent reader," and "[t]he solution must seem inevitable once revealed."

So much emphasis is placed on the revelation at the end of the penultimate chapter of *Watchmen* – the line "I did it thirty-five minutes ago" becoming one of the most notable quotes from the series – that it needs to be given careful scrutiny. Adrian Veidt's explanation for his actions works on more than one level: on the micro level, we have the murder of Edward Blake, the beginning of this mystery; on the macro level, we have the greater plan which required Blake's death to proceed. Both levels are linked, but they require different explanations and produce differing levels of belief in the reader. In order to believe the solution to the murder of Blake, one must grasp and believe in Veidt's greater plan. Moore takes a bold chance on tying a simple murder to the larger scheme; Chandler's three essential elements to a murder solution demonstrate how the entire story could fall apart here.

What Chandler means by simplicity has nothing to do with length. Rather, "[t]he ideal denouement is one in which everything is revealed in a flash of action" and is "something the reader is anxious to hear, and not a new story with a new set of characters, dragged in to justify an overcomplicated plot." The easiest way to judge the simplicity of this plot is to summarize it: Veidt killed Blake because the latter had stumbled onto his plot to kill a sizable portion of New York. Of course, the actual plot is far more detailed and is told over a much larger space... but at its heart, that is the solution to Blake's murder, and it is simple. Even so, the larger mystery that relates to Veidt's staged assassination attempt, the framing of Rorschach, and the other odd occurrences, still needs simplicity to make the dénouement work. Veidt's plan serves as the impetus for everything up until that point and is equally simple, explained in the same manner as Blake's killing. I have already argued that Veidt's motivation is believable, so that motivation spurring the rest of the action is also believable and simple to explain.

A solution being simple does not mean that it is stupid, though; Chandler also requires that the solution "must baffle a reasonably intelligent reader." Chandler recognizes that this is not always an essential part of a mystery story; even the best detective stories do not keep the reader in the dark until the end, "[b]ut there must be some important elements of the story that elude the most penetrating reader." In *Watchmen*'s case, it is safe to say the solution to Blake's murder almost certainly baffles an intelligent reader. Adrian Veidt kills Edward Blake to prevent Blake from blabbing about Veidt's plot to save the world from nuclear war with a fake alien? I highly doubt anyone comes to that conclusion ahead of time, because it is pretty far-fetched until spelled out. In fact, it is so far-fetched and so unsolvable ahead of time that the solution to Blake's murder does not seem to satisfy Chandler's requirements.

The solution to Blake's murder does not seem inevitable because it is so shocking. While Veidt's motivation and plan makes complete sense and appropriate clues are provided throughout, the solution is of the sort that only makes sense once you know it. Developing a solution that seems inevitable once revealed is one of the most difficult aspects of a mystery unless the writer is willing to sacrifice the actual mystery. Keeping the solution a secret and simultaneously making the solution so fantastically obvious in retrospect that the reader will smack his or her head for not having seen it coming is incredibly difficult. Here, the scope of the underlying mystery is so large that nothing about it seems inevitable. But framing the solution as a hero trying to save the world through unorthodox means does come close to fulfilling this requirement.

For his eleventh note, Chandler addresses a point similar to that of his sixth note:

> [The mystery story] must not try to do everything at once. If it is a puzzle story operating in a rather cool, reasonable atmosphere, it cannot also be a violent adventure or a passionate romance. An atmosphere of terror destroys logical thinking; if the story is about the intricate psychological pressures that lead apparently ordinary people to commit murder, it cannot then switch to the cool analysis of the police investigator. The detective cannot be hero and menace at the same time; the murderer cannot be a tormented victim of circumstance and also a heavy.

This note is problematic for *Watchmen*, which tells a big story. It does a great job of combining different types of story by firmly attaching those types to specific characters. For Rorschach, it's a mystery; for Nite Owl, it's an adventure; for Veidt, it's a quest; and so on. But does it try to do too much? Is it too busy, too unfocused? I think it works, but others could reach a different interpretation. This is the one note I cannot address conclusively, because the answer is very subjective.

For his final note, Chandler argues that, by the end of the story, the criminal must face a punishment of some sort, legal or otherwise. Chandler emphasizes that this is not for the sake of morality but because storytelling logic demands a resolution of the events or leaves the reader unsatisfied. There is no question that Moore does this, though by unconventional means; the resolution is implied but left unstated. At the end of *Watchmen*, we see Veidt facing his own conscience and doubt – unsure if he did the right thing, unsure whether the ends really do justify the means. Wanting to believe he acted correctly, he seeks validation from Dr. Manhattan. Instead, Dr. Manhattan adds a worse punishment when he points out that nothing ever ends: Veidt must confront that no matter how many times he saves the world, eventually he will not be around. He has not dispelled nuclear tensions so much as set them back. Solving one crisis does not prevent future ones from arising. And the very closing page suggests that even this success may come undone: Veidt's deeds in saving the world may yet be exposed after all.

Despite not fulfilling every requirement of Chandler's first twelve notes, Moore does adhere to the vast majority of them. However, Chandler came to feel some areas had been left unexplored in his original essay, so he added 13 more notes at later dates to cover other aspects of the story he missed with the initial dozen. Chandler's first addendum is less a requirement and more a recognition of fact: "The perfect detective story cannot be written. The type of mind which can evolve the perfect problem is not the type of mind that can produce the artistic job of writing." This addendum justifies a given story not fulfilling every condition Chandler had previously offered, since they do at times have conflicting requirements.

In the case of *Watchmen*, Moore's inability to make the solution seem inevitable is the result of his desire for a big, surprising revelation that alters the entire scope of the story. The scale of this revelation makes *Watchmen* better than it would have been otherwise, even at the cost of dramatic inevitability. Moore breaks the rule in order to make the story better, something Chandler knew and acknowledged was necessary. While we examine *Watchmen* here as a mystery story, it is far more than that, using the detective story as a jumping-off point for broader concerns, and this too requires deviating from the pure mystery story. That Moore is able to spend so much time outside of the mystery and still satisfy so many of Chandler's notes is remarkable.

One of the main reasons Moore is able to pull off the big reveal is because he hides the real mystery behind a false one. Rorschach's false assumption that Blake's murder is part of a plot to kill costumed heroes is the false mystery, encouraged and built up by Veidt to hide the true mystery. This false mystery fools the readers as well as Rorschach, making both parties focus on solving the wrong problem. We as readers follow Rorschach down the wrong path, delving too much into Blake's life and giving a false impression as to the motive behind his killing.

Chandler's third addenda note is that the reader should care about the corpse. Moore and Gibbons do their best to make sure that happens. But do we truly care about Edward Blake? We learn a lot about him as the story progresses. At first, we know he's a costumed hero of some sort, and that may win our sympathies quickly, particularly if we are already readers of super-hero comics – but then we learn about his attempted rape of another hero, which makes him repulsive. By the end of the story, we have gathered so much information about him and his life from so many perspectives that it is hard not to care about him on some level, even if only as a function of sheer familiarity.

Chandler's fourth addenda note is a simple statement that "Flip dialogue is not wit." Moore's dialogue is rarely flip. This is exceedingly rare for a super-hero comic of that time, especially one with such heavy noir overtones and with a detective as one of the main characters. Many writers would have given in to the temptation to write in an arch or pastiche style, reflecting the cliches commonly associated with that genre. Since Moore tries to write outside of the genre, placing the story in a more realistic world, he avoids many genre conventions in how characters speak.

Another way in which *Watchmen* is constructed that sets it apart from other comics of its time is that it functions equally well both in serialized form and as a collected volume. Looking at the crime and mystery magazines of an earlier era, Chandler noted in his addenda how mystery serials that relied on cliffhangers to hook readers at the end of each installment lost all their suspense when collected in book form. While originally serialized over 12 issues that kept readers in suspense, *Watchmen* has existed for 20 years as a collected edition and continues to sell steadily in this form.

The sixth and seventh addenda address the use of a love interest in a mystery story. Chandler emphasizes that a love interest weakens most mystery stories, but since Rorschach has no love interest, these particular notes are not applicable to *Watchmen* in that sense. Their closest application is to Nite Owl, who acts as a secondary detective – and it's highly interesting that he doesn't really focus on solving the mystery until the object of his affections, Silk Spectre, is temporarily removed from the scene.

In his sixth note, though, Chandler says something that also works with the eighth note. Chandler comments that a detective should never get married, because if he were to marry, "[h]e would lose his detachment, and this detachment is part of his charm"; in the eighth note, he adds that "[t]he hero of the mystery story is the detective. Everything hangs on his personality." The detachment Chandler discusses is actually a major part of Rorschach's personality; he maintains an objective viewpoint throughout the story, albeit one informed heavily by his own subjective view of morality. He is easily dismissive of those who do not conform to his idea of right and wrong. Rorschach's unique methods and approach makes him one of the most popular characters in *Watchmen*, fitting his role as the central detective in a mystery story.

The ninth and eleventh notes all touch on the criminal and some of the rules of how he is portrayed. Chandler argues that the "criminal cannot be the detective" and that he cannot be insane, since "[t]he murderer is not a murderer unless he commits murder in the legal sense." Neither of which apply to *Watchmen* since Rorschach is the detective and Veidt is not insane. The idea is broached, but his actions are too calculated and purposeful to be the work of a madman. At the end of the story, Moore plays with the notion that, while Rorschach is the detective and Veidt is the culprit, because Veidt's actions had altruistic motivations and Rorschach refuses to support them, perhaps Rorschach is the villain and Veidt the hero after all.

In the tenth, twelfth, and thirteenth addenda notes, Chandler raises some interesting points that apply tangentially to *Watchmen*. The tenth discusses first-person narration, which shows up in *Watchmen* in four instances: Rorschach's journal, the "Black Freighter" narration, the notes of Rorschach's psychiatrist, and Dr. Manhattan's narration of his life story. However, the only narration truly applicable to Chandler's intent is that in Rorschach's journal where he holds nothing back, as Chandler desires.

The thirteenth note deals with a convention of both mystery stories and super-hero comics; the audience knows the hero is never in any true danger, so building suspense is difficult. Moore and Gibbons deflect this concern in *Watchmen* from the start by beginning it with the death of a hero. On top of this, they further subvert that expectation at the end when Rorschach, the detective, is killed. *Watchmen* plays with genre conventions and audience expectations, so it exists both within the genre and outside of it at the same time.

Chandler's twelfth addendum returns to his first, offering another explanation for why the perfect mystery story is not possible, owing to the variety of readers and the simple fact that not all of them can be satisfied simultaneously. Chandler breaks down mystery readers into four types:

> The puzzle addict, for instance, regards the story as a contest of wits between himself and the writer; if he guesses the solution, he has won, even though he could not document his guess or justify it by solid reasoning. There is something of this competitive spirit in all readers, but the reader in whom it predominates sees no value beyond the game of guessing the solution. There is the reader, again, whose whole interest is in sensation, sadism, cruelty, blood, and the element of death. Again there is some in all of us, but the reader in whom it predominates will care nothing for the so-called deductive story, however meticulous. A third class of reader is the worrier-about-the-characters; this reader doesn't care so much about the solution; what really gets her upset is the chance that the silly little heroine will get her neck twisted on the spiral staircase. Fourth, and most important, there is the intellectual literate reader who reads mysteries because they are almost the only kind of fiction that does not get too big for its boots. This reader savors style, characterization, plot twists, all the virtuosities of the writing much more than he bothers about the solution. You cannot satisfy all these readers completely. To do so involves contradictory elements. I, in the role of reader, almost never try to guess the solution to a mystery. I simply don't regard the contest between the writer and myself as important. To be frank[,] I regard it as the amusement of an inferior type of mind.

And here we may have found a clue to the secret of *Watchmen*'s lasting success and extraordinary reputation. *Watchmen* is that rare story containing elements that target each of these types of reader. Blake's murder satisfies the puzzle addict, as does the revelation of Veidt's plot, which allows this type of reader to go back and discover all the clues missed in the first reading. From the opening panels of Blake's demise, the story contains rather graphic violence, including Rorschach's fight with the police, the prison riot, Blake's actions in Vietnam, and many others, satisfying the second type of reader. The third type is satisfied by the richness of the characters, but Rorschach's "cape killer" theory seemingly puts each of them in constant danger, allowing for the "worrier-about-the-characters" reader to find plenty of thrills throughout. Finally, Moore and Gibbons' technical prowess, their playing with genre convention, their experimental storytelling techniques, and the overall level of sophistication, and *Watchmen* cannot help but truly satisfy Chandler's fourth type of reader.

While Alan Moore may never have read Raymond Chandler's "Twelve Notes on the Mystery Story" when constructing the plot of *Watchmen* or the character of Rorschach, he comes very close to satisfying all of Chandler's requirements. Where Moore falls short it is not always because of a lack of skill but the result of purposeful choices, reflected in the inherent contradictions within Chandler's notes. All in all, the mystery of Edward Blake's murder is a compelling and engaging plot that stands along some of the best mystery stories ever written, with Rorschach taking his place alongside such notable detectives as Sherlock Holmes, Sam Spade, and Philip Marlowe.

Work Cited
Chandler, Raymond. "Twelve Notes on the Mystery Story." The Notebooks of Raymond Chandler. Ed. Frank MacShane. New York: Harper Perennial, 2006.

At Play Amidst the Strangeness and Charm: *Watchmen* and the Philosophy of Science

by William Ritchie

40 years. That's how long historian Max Weber claimed it took for "elite" scientific and philosophical ideas to filter down into the public consciousness. Of course, Weber's supposition is just another idea among ideas, so it may be as wrong as any of them. Still, let's play with this for a moment and see what it has to offer us.

40 years after Einstein's publication of the magical fact that $E=mc^2$, the Atomic Age arrived in twin bursts of light over Japan, bringing the awful, unforgettable knowledge of the mushroom cloud and the burnt shadows on the wall.

10 years after that, on the 40th anniversary of the publication of General Relativity, we were well into the grand age of American science-fiction: gravity, lightspeed, and space-time were understood well enough to serve as more than just arbitrary settings for symbolic drama but as integrated elements of the theme of Fate, too. Sci-fi was filled with Colossal Men and Shrinking Women, legions of mutated monsters, and super-heroes blighted by catastrophe and

accident but still striving to reassemble themselves into an ethical shape, framed against an impersonal universe. Not that we hadn't seen all this many times before, in the library of human storytelling, with the likes of Gilgamesh, Cuchullain, and Herakles. But that antique pattern of human fables and myth acquires a new *accent*, a new relevance, 40 years after Einstein. Suddenly, all at once, we were not just *homo sapiens* but *homo sapiens atomicus* – one step closer to the eschaton, and we knew it.

But in *Watchmen*, we can also *see* it: there are no images in the comic that are not weighted to exert this pressure on our reading. A dire presentiment is looming all around us, blowing us on into a final moment of revelatory conclusion we are not ready for – and do not want. The Comedian's murder (and murder mysteries are just local expressions of a grander philosophical struggle) starts a clock ticking. Someone is killing capes, and who's next? Well, the answer is that *we* are, as the profusion of interlinked symbols that fills the pages of *Watchmen* ceaselessly intimates to us the unavoidability of that final realization of entropy. War, and death, and chaos...

Or what is perhaps worse, *not* chaos at all but order. An implacable order that we can't resist; a pattern we're trapped in that we can't see. A group of people converge at a busy intersection in Manhattan just before a monumental crime to surpass Hiroshima takes place, with none of them having any idea how completely their lives are intertwined with the fate about to befall them.

Jon Osterman steps into an "Intrinsic Field Subtractor" and dies. What else can happen when all that is *intrinsic* to a living, breathing human being is stripped away from him? Good-natured Wally Weaver explains it to Jon in 1959. "What if there's some field holdin' stuff together, apart from gravity?" This shows us why he's just an assistant, because it's a shockingly inaccurate thing to say from a scientific perspective. There is no such thing in science as an "Intrinsic Field" nor any subtractor to remove it. Yet as it turns out, scientific inaccuracy notwithstanding, Wally's right. There *is* something that holds everything together.

It's called *meaning*.

Meaning is the ultimate goal of all our science, religion, and even our murder mysteries and science-fiction stories... but it's a very difficult goal to attain. "Meaning" is an abstraction, and we are none of us abstract creatures. For us, meaning is a matter of concrete objects, people, things, events, attributes, details, facts, and the endless attempt to know what things are *in themselves*. Somewhere beyond the approximations of our theories – all of which we have to trade in when they become obsolete, only to get new theories that will become obsolete in their turn – beyond all our *ideas* about the world, we believe there to be a "real" truth we would like to be able to reach out and touch, grasp, and hold.

But when Jon steps into the Intrinsic Field Subtractor in the lab at Gila Flats, that's all taken away from him. "The light... the light is taking me to pieces." And what residue can possibly be left? Like anyone else, Jon Osterman's identity lay in all that was intrinsic to him as an individual human person. He had a father, he had friends, he liked to fix watches, and he accepted glasses of cold beer from exciting women. His life was really just beginning; he had a future and a meaning all his own. Just as we all do, until death peels them away and we stop *being* anything – until we vanish from the world and stop being real.

In Jon's case, however, his departure from the world goes beyond the tragedy of death and on into something more terrible still: philosophy. He does not lose his "intrinsic nature" because he dies, but dies because it is removed from him – and how is he to do anything else then but cease? When the blue being called "Dr. Manhattan" returns to the world, it really is as no more than an abstraction of the man he was. Shorn of naturally-existing qualities, he is only a human being in schematic; an outline, a sketch. Like Leonardo's Vitruvian Man, Dr. Manhattan is not a person so much as something like an artwork or a memory. A ghost. Signal without carrier; a mere *idea*. It is the most horrible thing that could ever happen to a person, and the detachment of his internal monologue makes us feel it: the loss of a unique human soul to the heartless realms of pure theory.

And it's here that our story begins.

Many authors have attempted to present the implications of our own scientific knowledge and have missed the target, preferring not to see that what science and philosophy describe is the basis of the drama of our lives, not just convenient intellectual set-dressing. But in *Watchmen*, this is never forgotten, and Jon's accident is, in this regard, exemplary. The "pieces" of which he speaks are the subatomic particles whose behavior the branch of physics known as quantum mechanics has attempted to explain since the mid-1920s. Quantum uncertainty! Exclusion! The collapse of the wave function! But then again, they are not *just* that, because they are also symbols of the postmodern cultural theory that, from its emergence in the 1960s, has attempted to transform the scientific worldview of quantum mechanics into a social, literary, and philosophical aesthetic.   And you'll notice that there's roughly 40 years separating the birth of quantum theory from its adoption by philosophers and cultural theorists.

The last thing I'd expect would be for a postmodern philosopher to characterize his field as essentially "trickled-down" from decades old physics, just on Max Weber's say-so! But as we saw in the examples with Einstein, the 40-year conceit makes for an intriguing connection. A central idea of the quantum-mechanical worldview is that definite qualities are *not* intrinsic to the objects that possess those qualities, and therefore those objects can't be described as what they really are in themselves – because they are not really *anything* in themselves.   In this view, objects are only a set of statistical likelihoods – a cloud of qualities-in-potential, yet to be distilled into any specific form. We can never simply *find out* what they are, because their attributes are unfixed until we observe them. They're nothing without us. Well, that's a *very* simplified version of the theory, but it's all we need for our purposes. Max Weber would no doubt notice at least a surface similarity with postmodern literature, where meanings are volatile, motivations are occluded, and morals are evanescent. In this literature, *reading* is a far more important activity than writing: the central idea being that there is no such thing as an authoritative meaning possessed by a given text, only different ways of interpreting it, and none is privileged over any other.

Because nothing is intrinsic. *"The light is taking me to pieces."* But perhaps "pieces" are all Jon ever was – and all *any* of us are... just interchangeable pieces that carry meanings to and fro without ever really owning them. So all is illusion anyway, and meaning is just something detachable. Jon Osterman only *thinks* he's real and thinks that his story is his own... until time runs out, and he's shown it isn't and never was. He was only *ever* an idea; a ghost, a sketch.

The search for meaning may be difficult – even, in some sense, impossible – but that's very far from saying it's futile. The treatment of scientific concepts in *Watchmen* is so impressive in part because the treatment of it by others in the same vein has been so shortsighted. Seeming to regard it only as a tool for adducing   a   Rorschach-like   conclusion   about   the   world's   essential meaninglessness, other works have usually glossed over their own cosmological ambition, which is still to reach out and touch some real *truth*.

The postmodern suggestion that science itself is a social construction, subject to the "reading" of different political and cultural interpretations, is far from an improper one, but the assumption that postmodernism can wield science's own authority in making that case *against* it is certainly illegitimate. Quantum-mechanical researchers themselves, if exposed to this view, usually bristle and tell the postmodernists that they have simply got what they took from science all *wrong*. They might tell the postmodernists that they have forgotten, if you like, the blood that was drawn from the shoulder of Pallas.

But then again, science itself sometimes makes that same mistake, too.

> The philosopher and an elderly lady argue: the philosopher says the world is a globe that orbits the sun, but the woman says the world is a flat plate, supported on the backs of four elephants standing underneath it.
>
> "But what are the elephants standing on?" the philosopher wants to know. "They are standing on something, I presume?"
>
> The woman replies: "Well, of course they are! They're standing on the back of a giant turtle."
>
> "Aha!" the philosopher says, "but then what's the turtle standing on?"
>
> His interlocutor thinks a moment, and then offers the suggestion that the turtle is standing on yet another, bigger turtle.
>
> "I see!" returns the philosopher mildly. "But then what is *that* turtle standing on?"
>
> The old lady wags her finger at him. "You're very clever, young man, very clever... but you can't trick *me!* It's turtles all the way down!"

In some versions of that story, the philosopher in question is said to be Bertrand Russell. In other versions, he is William James. It never happened, of course. Nonetheless, it's a very useful story. When we look at Jon's accident, we should realize that we are looking not at a technical device, but at a *literary* one. Jon doesn't say, "I am being separated into my constituent subatomic particles" any more than he says "I am having my human specificity removed from me." The Intrinsic Field Subtractor is a pseudo-scientific dream machine of the type common to sociological science-fiction. Like faster-than-light propulsion or time machines or universal translators, it is not there to lend verisimilitude but to get the plot to a place where its central conflicts can be intelligibly worked out. Moore and Gibbons are not telling us anything definite about the connection between quantum mechanics and postmodern philosophy – they are not trying to tell their story by expounding upon what reality *is*. Rather, they are only directing us to the site of human conflict with what it *may be*. Through pseudo-scientific metaphor, they raise the question of just what these two real-life theories may have to do with one another, but they don't answer it.

This is wise, because the entire nature of theories is that they are problematic. They will all have to be thrown out one day, remember? Them and their turtles too. That no theory is forever means no theory is authoritative, and so in a certain sense it *is* how you come at the world that determines what meaning you will see in it. Blood from the shoulder of Pallas? In science, the most *real* thing there is, is the difficulty of getting our fingers close enough to Truth that we can touch it. The postmodern philosophers are not entirely wrong about the character of that endeavor, because *doing science* means indulging beliefs that are all but guaranteed to end up proven utterly false. So if we already know our belief is going to be proven false when we choose it, why *do* we choose it? Why *should* we choose it? Why should we ever prefer one belief to another at all? Where do our "elite" ideas even *come* from, anyway?

Perhaps the central preoccupation of the academic field called History and Philosophy of Science ("HPS" for short) is the idea that we've got our history of ideas all wrong, in that we tend to talk about them as though they existed apart from the people who *had* them. An absurd thought, but at the same time, a seductive one. It gives us a reason to believe the confusing disarray of our present can be explained as something that's developed out of simpler actors than ourselves, and according to a rationally-comprehensible plan that, from our more advanced position, we can decode with a satisfying assurance. In pursuit of this assurance, we find it convenient to regard the people of the past as mere flotsam in the river of historical trends, passing ideas from hand to hand without ever making them. The truth is that people *do* make ideas, and we just don't like to think about it. The odd "Great Man" standing like a mighty boulder in the current of events we can tolerate, but to assign a full intellectual agency to *all* the dwellers in the past would be to make the past too complex for our comfort. After all, if we make every molecule of the stream a Great Man, mustn't we entirely give up the idea of a current, abandon all generalizations, and relinquish every hope of meaning? And then where would we be?

Where do our elite ideas come from? They are really not elite at all, because they come from *everybody* desperate to understand their world more fully, who's ever grabbed from this and stolen from that in an effort to cobble together some symbol of the world. True, no one but Einstein ever gave us the famous rubber sheet of space-time, and no one but Bohr and Heisenberg ever gave us the mysterious collapse of the wave function... and these elite *symbols* of our scientific knowledge are so valuable as to be beyond price. But their value doesn't change the fact that Einstein wasn't the *first* person to think about the nature of time, anymore than Heisenberg and Bohr were the first to think about how the observer is part of the system he is attempting to measure.

And that's what makes *Watchmen* such a marvel; that it shows us *precisely* this, and *just* this, and leaves it all in our laps. Here is not just a universe established by authorial fiat – *"This book will be in the postmodern style...!"* – in order to prop up some pet cosmological theory, but instead one that grapples with the very real difficulty of attempting to do so in the first place. Therefore, even if we label it "postmodern science fiction," we must concede it comes by that label honestly. Of all the coincidences, synchronicities, and indicators of infinite connection *Watchmen* shows us, there is not a single one that, if seen from another angle or in another slice of time or simply in another order, would not miss its synchronistic connection. Laurie's remark about fog would not coincide with her face being obscured by the steam of Dan's kettle; her posture would not reflect the Comedian's stance of a decade earlier, as she and Dan head to the fire.

And yet, those connections would all still *be* there, strewn across the pages of the narrative like Rorschach's sugar cubes. And that's the point of this miracle; perhaps we wouldn't be so fortunate as to *notice* them, but they would be *there*. The coincidences in *Watchmen*'s world are (for want of a better word) *real* coincidences. There is nothing we are not intensely familiar with in the way they line up to offer possible meanings that nevertheless remain subliminal to the characters they cluster around. Because we're well aware that's what the elements of our *own* lives are wont to do.

In HPS, Newton's apple is the sovereign symbol of understanding. Not because it symbolizes his theory of gravitation, but because it symbolizes the way scientific theories assemble themselves out of what is already known. A theory is *discovered*, in a flash, as the pattern we already knew pulls itself together and drops down on our heads out of a clear blue sky. It's the same with our theories of history that – once they fall on our heads – instantly recontextualize past events. Stories of development we once believed explode before our eyes to reassemble themselves into new patterns, new causes for the effect known as *us*. Patterns which, we are suddenly tempted to believe, we always recognized deep down. And maybe we did. "Professor Einstein says that time differs from place to place," Jon's father tells him in 1945. "Can you imagine?" Of course the tragedy is that Jon *can* but doesn't know it yet. 40 years later, the meteors rain down on Mars, with perfect implacability.

For all that, *Watchmen* is easily the most responsible and relevant incorporation of genuine real-world science into a fictional narrative I've ever encountered – without question, it remains the "hardest" science-fiction story I have ever read – paradoxically, there is only one moment in the entire series in which anyone even tries to *do* anything like "real" science. And it is over so quickly.

Dr. Manhattan turns down Laurie's implied invitation to a reunion dinner with Dan Dreiberg, saying, "I'd join you, but I think I'm close to locating a gluino, which would completely validate supersymmetrical theory if we could include it in the bestiary." And this is absolutely true. Supersymmetry predicts each standard particle has a corresponding hypothetical superpartner. The purported superpartner of the gluon would be a gluino. No gluino has ever been observed, but if one were, superstring theory would be confirmed.

But because of what he says, she leaves and he stays. And because of the kind of story this is, we follow her and not him. Whereupon the story becomes an endless parade of pseudo-scientific literary devices not unlike the Intrinsic Field Subtractor. Spark hydrants, telepathy, instantaneous teleportation, bullet-catching, geomantic TV-watching, hover-scooters, big-eared lynxes, tachyon-emitters, Owl-ships, and a somewhat fanciful idea of how computer passwords work – all quite beautiful as metaphors and all quite impossible. But the impossibility itself accomplishes something a more realistic salting of science most definitely would not: it lets us see both how disturbing these juvenile metaphorical violations are – and how ultimately pointless.

A little while later in the narrative, a glass beaker breaks, spilling liquid everywhere. Dr. Manhattan, in absolute contradiction of all that is thermodynamic, calmly reassembles all the relevant molecules into their previous positions... and presto! The accident is undone. It's the very essence of the jarring, frightening madness of "super-powers" – those paradoxical and extra "powers" that explode definitions by being able to do thoroughly impossible work. To unboil the water by turning up the heat! However, the exhibition of super-powers fails to represent *freedom* as it normally would in a comic-book narrative. Despite the spookiness of Dr. Manhattan's ability, it is only another literary device.

And what's more to the point, the reversal of entropy is a *local* effect only. A broken beaker is put back together, seemingly in defiance of the grand Humpty-Dumpty principle of the arrow of time; but as with much in *Watchmen*, this local miracle is only symptomatic of a wider incapacity – the backhanded proof of a more universal failure. The irony of placing the device of "super-powers" in a real-world setting only highlights a more primal helplessness in the face of the larger forces of Time and Fate. No matter what we do, we cannot change the way things are. No matter what we do – and no matter how successfully we do it – we cannot keep the *consequence* of time from existing. Even if our ideas about what time is are completely wrong, there is no super-power that can make us truly free of time.

Physicists today seek pantingly after evidence of that same supersymmetrical jewel of time that Dr. Manhattan is imprisoned in – and a single gluino is all it would take to put us all in there with him. But implicit in their search is the cosmic futility that Jon knows very well: because the world is still the world no matter *what* we do to it. No matter how many extra dimensions we imagine it having, we will never be able to imagine enough of them to escape the way its randomness and its irreversibility eventually unmakes all our meanings. Signs and symbols are constantly boiling out of space-time all around us, but like the gluino, they're too evanescent for us to pin down.

At some point or other, most of the characters in *Watchmen* have their philosophies deeply wounded by an encounter with the Comedian. Standing before his burnt map in 1966, Nelson Gardner realizes that his strategy has grown as irrelevant as his worldview. Under fireworks in Vietnam in 1971, Jon Osterman learns that his notions of his own humanity have their limit. In the riots of 1977, Dan Dreiberg's idealism is fatally punctured. On Mars in 1985, Laurie Juspeczyk learns the story of her identity is built entirely from lies. And the Comedian spurs Adrian Veidt's master plan.

Each one of the other characters is assaulted and then in some sense retires from belief. Their efforts to make sense of their world are defeated by the Comedian's energetic, amoral honesty. In a way, this is the lesson of *Watchmen* in a nutshell: our theories about the world are partly projected

The reversal of entropy is a local effect only. From *Watchmen* #3 (November 1986). Copyright © DC Comics.

from inside us, not entirely from outside. They are as much reflections of our fallible desire, as of our experience.

But Adrian, as "the world's smartest man," alone chooses to parse this lesson another way. Rather than retire from his position when confronted with its failure, he instead recommits to it with a fanatic's severity. It's true that he doesn't really *sound* to us like a fanatic, but that's only because his belief is such a familiar one. Because it's the idea of *progress* that forms Adrian's sovereign philosophical symbol: the belief in history as a statistical drive from the simple and primitive to the complex and civilized in a crooked but constantly upward-tending graph of Net Good, just like the stock market. Which is also a model that, coincidentally, makes the one who recapitulates the progress of human advancement in his *own* life the one who is truly Great: the self-made man as the very icon of Perfectability. The top of the pyramid.

However, it's a more precarious perch than it seems. Adrian's creed may be rational, but it is mad too; although he tries to take his justification from a vision of science, his actions are actually founded on the *myth* of science, the myth of a simple past. To Jon, there's no such thing as the past. There is only the eternal present, in which nothing is "simple" but all is infinitely involved.

As failures of perspective go, Adrian sets new records. His *jejune* apologies for mass murder are horrifying: "People died... perhaps unnecessarily, though who can judge such things?" But Adrian's fault doesn't lie in his puerile ethic alone but in the fact that it is inseparable from his shortcomings as a philosopher. But was there ever a mass-murderer on his scale not motivated by some inept philosophy or other? His simplistic view of history as the story of Great Men – like believing the planets are the biggest things in the sky, because they're the closest – is one with his stubbornly Newtonian view of time as something calculable. The analysis of events, the extrapolation of trends, allows him as the exemplary individual to divine what's on the other pages of the universe's book without having to turn them... and so choose when and how to intervene.

But in the age of quantum mechanics, such a view is hopelessly antique, and the sooner we recognize it the better... because from our perspective, that theory of knowledge is just another burnt map. To Jon as to us, it isn't that you can divine what's on the other pages without having to turn them but that everything is on every page, all the time, continuously. And you can't *not* intervene, because to see *is* to intervene.

Inevitably, the climax comes: Adrian attempts to defend himself from Dr. Manhattan by turning another Intrinsic Field Subtractor on him. And it's an absolutely woeful failure, because Adrian thinks Jon still has an Intrinsic Field to *lose*.

Of course he doesn't; that idol has already fallen. *And behold, the door is open, and the knot is untied!* Unfortunately, Adrian cannot bring himself to abandon the obsolete formula in which the meanings of all things may be comprehended and tamed by the superior intellect. And so, he seeks to triumph over Jon by taking his potent, current-deflecting *super-specialness* away from him... unable to see that Jon had lost it long since. And his tragedy is that he can never get it back, if it even once existed.

So, poor Adrian! His egoistical worldview can't tolerate this irreducible human implication, so again he doesn't see: to conquer what Jon represents, he'd need a much bigger dream-machine than a mere Intrinsic Field Subtractor. He would need an equally nonexistent Intrinsic Field *Generator*, a magical device capable of supplying meanings that *should* be there but aren't.

But of course, there are no meanings that "should" be anywhere. No more than water can be *unboiled*, instead of steaming away from us at 40 years per second.

Blotting out Reality: Questioning Rorschach

by Gene Phillips

> They had a choice, all of them. They could have followed the footsteps of good men like my father, or President Truman. Decent men who believed in a day's work for a day's pay. Instead they followed the droppings of lechers and Communists and didn't realize that the trail led over a precipice until it was too late.
> — *Watchmen*, Chapter I, page 1

> Existence is random. Has no pattern save what we imagine after staring at it for too long. No meaning save what we choose to impose.
> — *Watchmen*, Chapter VI, page 26

Despite the emphasis on "choice" in both passages, the statements above seem to come from two separate people. The first statement is that of a fervent ultra-conservative, a believer in the fundamental good of the capitalist work-ethic and the evils of self-indulgence and socialism. The second belongs to a nihilist with a strong Nietzschean bent; a nihilist whose only belief is that no human value is anything more than an illusion projected upon a meaningless void.

Yet both statements come from the character of Rorschach, whose voice is the first one the reader encounters in *Watchmen*. Seeing these statements juxtaposed, the reader might speculate that the speaker made them at radically different times in his life. But the statements appear within about two weeks of each other, within the story's principal timeline, in the year 1985 (one year before *Watchmen* was first published as a periodical mini-series). This leads to two questions. First, can it be demonstrated that there are not one but two Rorschachs in *Watchmen*? And second, how does that incongruity affect the philosophical themes of the work?

Before addressing either question, it must be said that this apparent incongruity does not spring from *Watchmen*'s collaborative process. When artist and writer collaborate on a comics work, an artist's visual cues may undercut the original intention of the writer, or the writer may interpolate verbal information into a drawn panel without consulting the artist. But Rorschach's schizophrenia is not cued by the art of Dave Gibbons. Visually, the Rorschach who rants against Communists has the same appearance and body language as the Rorschach who declares that existence is random. The two Rorschachs, then, arise purely from discontinuities in Alan Moore's script and must be addressed as the result of Alan Moore's contradictory philosophical concerns.

Watchmen offers an ironic take on the genre most associated with American comic books, that of the super-hero. Moore's liberal bent – which he repeatedly defined as "anarchist" in his many interviews – is plain from the satirical tone of the first quote, in which Rorschach rails against "lechers and Communists." The view that all super-hero stories were bastions of conservatism has since been challenged by Bradford Wright's critical tome *Comic Book Nation* (2001), but at the time Moore wrote *Watchmen*, that view was accepted wisdom. Moore's attitude toward mainstream super-heroes is implied by the nature of his original proposal: that he could take a group of long-unpublished super-heroes and rewrite them in more realistic terms. The project began with Moore's discussions with DC Comics about the possibility of his refurbishing a group of 1960s costumed heroes that DC had acquired from defunct publisher Charlton Comics. In the end, Moore took six Charlton heroes – Blue Beetle, Captain Atom, Nightshade, Thunderbolt, Peacemaker, and the Question – and used them as rough templates for six new characters: Nite Owl, Doctor Manhattan, Silk Spectre, Ozymandias, the Comedian, and Rorschach.

For the first five on that list, Moore does not make more than token reference to the characters on whom they were modeled. Moore's Ozymandias is a general critique of the "self-made man" type of hero, not specifically of Peter Morisi's character Thunderbolt; the Comedian is a parody of all patriotic heroes, not specifically of Pat Boyette's Peacemaker. But the case of Rorschach is different, for in Rorschach, Moore coded several references not just to the Charlton hero, but also to the larger oeuvre of Steve Ditko, the writer-artist who created the Question. Indeed, Rorschach is distinguished from the other characters in deriving elements from not one but two heroes created by Ditko in the same year, 1967 – one of whom was a "question," while the other was an "answer."

The early careers of Moore and Ditko have a few parallels to one another. Ditko drew comics for over ten years until gaining a measure of fame when he and Stan Lee co-created Spider-Man in 1962. Alan Moore worked in British comics for roughly four years before coming to the attention of American comics fandom with his work on *Swamp Thing* in the early 1980s. Additionally, Moore's resolve to use the genre of the super-hero to address complex social matters finds an ancestor in the work of Steve Ditko. Ditko walked away from Spider-Man in 1966, and in the following year created two characters that expressed more of his personal philosophy than Spider-Man had. The first, created for Charlton, was the Question (*Blue Beetle* #1, June 1967), while the second was Mister A, who first appeared in the independently-published alternative comic *witzend* and whose initial "A" signified "the answer," as in "Q & A." The design of Rorschach's costume draws on both characters, even as the two personas Moore gives to Rorschach embody different aspects of Moore's adversarial response to Steve Ditko.

Steve Ditko's philosophy does not admit easy summation, but one approach is to see it as an outgrowth of the tropes of the costumed crimefighter genre – tropes regarded as intrinsically "conservative" by Alan Moore, among others. The first Question story does follow those tropes yet also transforms them. Crusading telejournalist Vic Sage, who is also the costumed crimefighter the Question, uses his secret identity to seek a gambling czar who is guilty of murder. In most super-hero stories, the main point of the story would be to ferret out the lawbreaker, and Ditko does satisfy that narrative requirement. But Ditko devotes more space to showing the casual hypocrisy of the man in the street (who tolerates gambling) and of Sage's fellow journalists (who resent Sage's uncompromising attitude toward crime). Thus the story's problem becomes not just how to bring villains to justice, but also to ask "questions" as to what society should do in response to facts they may find unpleasant. Lack of compromise between good and evil became one of the hallmarks of the Ditko oeuvre, taking inspiration not from standard conservatism but from the Objectivist beliefs of Ayn Rand, which provided Ditko with his philosophical underpinnings.

In Mister A's first adventure, the title character is even more outspoken about the uncompromising nature of truth: "when one knows what is black, *evil,* from what is white, *good,* there can be no justification for choosing any part of evil."

In terms of physical appearance, Moore and Gibbons' Rorschach borrows from design elements found in both Ditko heroes – beginning with the conceit that all three characters wear suit-clothes rather than the super-hero's "long underwear." Of the three, only Mister A's suit has any extraordinary aspect: in keeping with Ditko's conceit that "white" means "good," the hero's suit and hat are all-white, as is the metal mask covering the hero's normal face. The crusader uses black only in the token with which he terrifies guilty criminals: a half-black and half-white calling card, denoting the total incommensurability of evil and good. But the dichotomy of black and white is Mister A's only strong influence on Rorschach, for Mister A's mask merely looks like an ordinary human face, albeit one fixed in a scornful expression.

In contrast, both the Question and Rorschach wear full face-masks that reveal no features whatsoever. But where the Question's mask is perfectly blank – making him the incarnation of what one might call "faceless justice" – Rorschach's white mask is covered with black blotches that resemble the inkblots of the famous psychological test. In conversation with his prison psychiatrist in Chapter VI, Rorschach explains that he liked the material from which he later makes his mask precisely because it separates the black and white from one another – just as one sees in the token of Mister A. But because the cloth is a science-fictional creation, the black blots on the mask are not fixed but mobile, constantly reconfiguring against the mask's white background. For both the Question and Rorschach, the featureless mask signifies that its wearer is removed from the need to use facial features to communicate affect. But for Ditko, the mask conveys that its wearer is the vehicle of a remorseless rationality; for Moore, the mask signifies that its wearer is dangerously psychotic.

As noted earlier, Moore's *raison d'être* in revising long-unpublished super-heroes was to show their limitations within a more realistic cosmos. Ditko's

Investigative journalist Vic Sage assumes a faceless visage as the Question, in his first appearance from *Blue Beetle* #1 (June 1967), with story and art by Steve Ditko. Copyright © DC Comics.

Mister A and the Charlton heroes have little or no backstory – and barely any character traits beyond the desire to serve justice. In contrast, all of Moore's *Watchmen* characters have intensely detailed biographies, some of which spill over from the story proper into documents that purport to explain each character's quirks and passions. Walter Kovacs (a.k.a. Rorschach) receives far more biographical attention than the other five, perhaps because he is the figure through which Moore attacks both the general "conservatism" of the super-hero genre and the specific philosophical concerns of Ditko.

According to Rorschach's prison psychiatrist, the crusader's motives come down to "misdirected aggression." Although *Watchmen* implies that the psychiatrist's verdict is superficial, Moore never explicitly contradicts this particular opinion. Most super-hero tales begin with the protagonist suffering injustice from crime or tyranny, then mounting a crusade against evil. But whereas most nascent heroes only need one injustice to motivate them, Walter Kovacs's very life is an injustice, starting from conception. Kovacs's mother, a small-time prostitute, conceives him with a man who leaves before Kovacs is born and whom Kovacs never meets. The only datum the mother gives her son about his absent father is that he liked President Truman, while she did not. Therefore, because Kovacs despises his mother for her dalliances with other men and for her physical abuse of him (recollected on page 4 of Chapter VI), Kovacs idealizes his absent father and conflates him with President Truman, as seen in the first quote. Thus, like the Ditko heroes, Kovacs formulates a strong opposition between good and evil, with evil represented not just by illegality but also by "lechery" and any form of bodily indulgence – also a symbol of his hated mother.

However, this ultraconservative persona remains dormant in Kovacs until 1964, when Kovacs reads about the murder of Kitty Genovese, witnessed by dozens of people who did nothing to stop it. This insight into human depravity inspires Kovacs to create a mask from the aforementioned "black blot" cloth, material which (very coincidentally) was intended for a dress ordered by Ms. Genovese. This mask, says Kovacs, gave him "a face that I could bear to look at in a mirror." Implicitly, such a face allows Kovacs to distance himself from common, sinful humanity, as do the visages of the Question and Mister A.

The reader only sees Rorschach's early incarnation once, in a flashback to 1966. Whereas the Rorschach seen in all of the 1985 scenes speaks in broken sentences and with an unnerving monotone, the 1966 Rorschach uses full sentences, and his word-balloons are not distorted like those of the 1985 version, signifying the absence of any spooky voice. Since the 1966 Rorschach is no less militant against evil than the later version, this early Rorschach may simply has better control of his demons – until the year 1975, which gives birth to the "nihilist Rorschach" persona, whose main purpose is to undermine Steve Ditko's Objectivist credo.

Most super-heroes only are created by trauma, but Rorschach also receives a trauma that very nearly uncreates him, removing most of his sanity. In 1975, Rorschach seeks to find a little girl, kidnapped by a man who mistook her for the daughter of rich parents. Rorschach's 1975 methods are nearly as extreme as they are a decade later; Rorschach describes how he "visited underworld bars and began hurting people. Put fourteen in hospital needlessly. Fifteenth gave me an address..." This address leads him to the kidnapper's home, but the hero is too late: the kidnapper has already disposed of the evidence by killing the little girl and feeding her body to his dogs. Rorschach kills both the kidnapper and the dogs; after that, it's said that his violence became more extreme. But it's noteworthy that he still doesn't take lives as promiscuously as the Comedian does (despite the fact that Rorschach admires the Comedian's lack of compromise). The reader is told only of one other criminal whom Rorschach actually murders – a multiple rapist, killed by Rorschach to signify the crusader's defiance of the Keene Act prohibiting costumed vigilantes. (Dan Dreiberg also claims that Rorschach once dealt with the masochistic Captain Carnage by dropping him down an elevator shaft, but the outcome of this encounter is unknown.) Rorschach remains the only vigilante who continues to operate against this law, which he does for another seven years before being caught. On the other hand, he also becomes an obsessive paranoid who speaks in sentence fragments and fails to bathe very often, if at all.

Just as Ditko's first Question story is far more focused upon a search for philosophical truth than the apprehension of a guilty criminal, Chapter VI of *Watchmen* (titled "The Abyss Gazes Also") is similarly constructed, though the truth finally reached is that there is no objective truth. The chapter's title is taken from an epigraph by Friedrich Nietzsche, reproduced at the chapter's end: "Battle not with monsters, lest ye become a monster. And if you gaze into the abyss, the abyss gazes also into you."

Appropriately, the book in which Nietzsche published this epigraph sounds like a virtual refutation of Steve Ditko: Nietzsche's book is titled *Beyond Good and Evil.* Alan Moore, however, was hardly making a systematic exploration of the Nietzschean philosophy. He merely utilized certain aspects of it to dispute Steve Ditko's regimented dichotomy between good and evil, rationality and irrationality.

There's no doubt that Chapter VI is one of the strongest sections of *Watchmen.* Moore incisively displays the insidious logic of Rorschach's pathology, which more or less "infects" his prison psychiatrist with a vision of "empty meaningless blackness." Nietzsche's image of "the abyss" – which matches the image of the black blots on Rorschach's mask – becomes a dominant trope in that chapter. After Rorschach makes his declaration about the randomness of existence, he continues, "The void breathed hard on my heart, turning its illusions to ice, shattering them. Was reborn then, free to scrawl own design on this morally blank world. Was Rorschach."

Rorschach claims that, prior to this negative epiphany, he was only "Kovacs pretending to be Rorschach." Yet this nihilist persona barely seems to exist outside of Chapter VI. If the 1975 Rorschach loses all of his illusions, why does the 1985 Rorschach rant against "liberals and intellectuals and smooth-talkers," if he really believes he inhabits a "morally blank world?" Seven years after Kovacs stopped "pretending to be Rorschach," the crimefighter is still subscribing to the right-wing magazine *New Frontiersman* and apparently takes its rhetoric seriously, even to the extent that he entrusts his private journal to the publication. When Silk Spectre accuses the late Comedian of having tried to rape her mother, Rorschach's reply is that of the staunch conservative reactionary: "I'm not here to speculate on the moral lapses of men who died in their country's service." To someone free of illusions, service to one's country should mean no more than not serving one's country.

Possibly Moore meant to suggest that after Rorschach saw the meaninglessness of existence, he fell back into the habits of his ultra-conservative persona. Moore hints at this possibility in one line on page five of Chapter X, where Rorschach tells Nite Owl that one can survive "on the edge" if "you observe rules." But this toss-off line isn't enough to render all of Rorschach's contradictory beliefs credible. In Chapter I, Rorschach wonders to himself if it makes sense to track down the Comedian's killer at a time when nuclear holocaust threatens the world, but he concludes with conservative rigor: "there is good and there is evil, and evil must be punished. Even in the face of Armageddon, I shall not compromise in this."

And yet, three days later in Chapter II, the vigilante speculates that he and all of his fellow crimefighters may be motivated by some sort of psychological determinism: "Something in our personalities, perhaps? Some animal urge to fight and struggle, making us what we are? Unimportant. We do what we have to do." Whatever the failings of Steve Ditko's philosophy, Ditko would have known that a belief in determinism was not easily reconciled with a belief in absolute good and absolute evil.

Having seen the discontinuities of the two Rorschachs, one must ask how successful Moore's response to Steve Ditko proves. In an interview in *Comic Book Artist* #9, conducted in June 2000, Moore drew attention to Ditko's "right-wing agenda" and observed, "that probably led to me portraying Rorschach as an extremely right-wing character." This confirms the aspect of "ultra-conservative Rorschach," but says nothing as to the more specific ways Moore responded to Ditko's Objectivist philosophy.

As noted earlier, Mister A's name connoted "the answer," but it also connotes the proposition "A=A," which Ayn Rand calls "the law of identity" in her book *For the New Intellectual*. She wrote, "Whatever you choose to consider, be it an object, an attribute, or an action, the law of identity remains the same. A leaf cannot be a stone at the same time; it cannot be all red and all green at the same time." Ditko, following in the footsteps of his philosophical mentor, applied the same "law of identity" to the question of good and evil, as in this lecture by Mister A (another telejournalist) to his television audience:

> A truth is truth for all, an absolute! To compromise, to give up any part of a truth is to wipe out justice, to choose some evil over the good, to renounce man's means, reason and logic which makes his success and happiness possible! Each man must make his own choice! A is A or *anything goes*!
> — *Mr. A* #2

For Ditko, "reason and logic" are the tools by which humankind knows truth. Both Ayn Rand and Steve Ditko tie this concept to a reification of conservative ideology, but both raise a valid philosophical question as to the value of man's rational faculties. It would be possible to answer Ditko's rational absolutism via Nietzschean philosophy, but Alan Moore didn't do this. Rather, Moore used Nietzsche to disassociate Rorschach from anything comparable to "reason and logic," which could be viewed as an evasion of the actual content of Ditko's philosophy. In fact, the "determinism" ruminations of Chapter II make Rorschach sound less like a Ditko hero than a Ditko villain – such as the character of "Our Man" in *Blue Beetle* #6 (November 1968) who feels himself "ruled by strange forces that control man's will and destiny."

Perhaps the greatest dichotomy between Moore's two Rorschachs appears at the conclusion of *Watchmen*, which is more emotionally satisfying than philosophically consistent. In brief, the rogue hero Ozymandias tells the remaining heroes that he has set into motion a plot to force Earth's warring nations to come together via a false threat of alien invasion. This is, in essence, the super-heroic version of Plato's "noble lie," in which a salient fact is suppressed in order to manipulate society for its own good. The other heroes agree to suppress the truth of Ozymandias's deception, in order to keep the nuclear powers from destroying the Earth, but Rorschach refuses to compromise with evil, and this brings about his own destruction by one of his former allies.

This is perhaps the one place where the persona of "nihilist Rorschach" comes closest to any of the Ditko heroes. Logically, "ultra-conservative Rorschach," who was willing to blink at the questionable deeds of a veteran soldier, should have been willing to go along with the deception. But "nihilist Rorschach" is not willing, for though he has no concept of Mister A's "reason and logic," he does emulate the Ditko hero's passionate hatred of evil, even when it purports to serve mankind. But even here, Moore breaks with Ditko tellingly: where Ditko's heroes wear masks that are true reflections of themselves, Rorschach's final act before dying is to divest himself of the mask that conceals all affect.

Even in the ranks of canonical literature, it's not unusual to find authors who depict characters with contradictory aspects. "Nihilist Rorschach" never melds with "ultra-conservative Rorschach," but Chapter VI remains one of the best things Alan Moore wrote. So perhaps we can live with the fact that the two personas don't meld any more than do the black and white patterns on the character's mask.

The Last Laugh: Understanding *Watchmen*'s Big Joke

by John Loyd

As a satirical re-imagining of life during the Cold War, *Watchmen* is one big joke. Of course, the work has several themes, major and minor, but one character embodies what is arguably its most important. He is the key to understanding the book and the manifestation of the makers' methods. He is Edward Blake, the Comedian. This essay explores his function in the text – and, hopefully, seeks to help you understand just what the big joke is.

Let's begin with a brief look at the world we're entering when we open *Watchmen*, which strays from the 1980s we might remember. It's a world of seemingly improved technology: electric hubs recharge cars, and blimps fill the sky like clouds. Politically, things are a bit different as well: thanks to Dr. Manhattan, the United States did not suffer the frustration of Vietnam, and the same blue bombshell also keeps foreign threats at bay. Life seems good. But despite the purported advances of mankind in *Watchmen*, its world is rather broken. One of the more poignant examples comes at the end of Chapter IV, in a text excerpt ostensibly written by Dr. Milton Glass: "Children starve while boots costing many thousands of dollars leave their mark upon the surface of the moon. We have labored long to build a heaven, only to find it populated with horrors." Farther down that page, Glass continues:

Never before has man pursued global harmony more vocally while amassing stockpiles of weapons so devastating in their effect. The Second World War – we were told – was The War to End Wars. The development of the atomic bomb is the Weapon to End Wars. And yet wars continue…

So perhaps, for all its technology, the world of *Watchmen* is not so fundamentally different from our own. Except, of course, that it is filled with masked heroes. To truly appreciate their presence, we must look at *Watchmen* as a situated text. Just as we would consider any other work of literature or cinema in light of the era and traditions from which it comes, *Watchmen* – like all sequential art, arguably – demands a cognizance of its place, a sort of comic-book exegesis, if you will.

Comic books have their own language – a jargon understood only by those deeply versed in sequential art. In *Understanding Comics: The Invisible Art*, Scott McCloud claims that the medium "offers range and versatility with all the potential imagery of film and painting plus the intimacy of the written word." Comics conglomerate all the aesthetics of the page. Layout of content within a panel, color, panel size and spacing between panels, text font: these are tools the comic creator holistically employs. Other media offer only one or a few of these elements. Comics draw on the synergy of them all working together. But one has to be able to understand their usage, because these elements are rarely used arbitrarily.

In *Watching the Watchmen,* colorist John Higgins describes the creators' intent when they were planning the book. "All along," he says, "Alan and Dave wanted *Watchmen* to be, visually, completely different from any other comic book that was around at that time, and of course, that we achieved." Dave Gibbons explains how they accomplished this, broadly speaking:

> I had an epiphany one day when I realized that *Watchmen* was not a super-hero book as such, but rather a work of science fiction, an alternate history. Accordingly, I was determined to make *Watchmen* look different from the super-hero comics of the time.

He elaborates, "I wanted them to be individuals, more like the caricatures common in European comics, rather than the square-jawed variations on a theme of most American comics."

Here is where things get really interesting. Often when we think of caricatures, we think of highly exaggerated features. Yet the *Watchmen* characters are not caricatures in this sense. In *Understanding Comics,* Scott McCloud explains how differences in gradations of reality affect reader identification with a character or environment. McCloud claims that the more *cartoonishly* a character is drawn, the more widely people will be able to connect or identify with that character. "For example, while most characters were designed simply, to assist in reader-identification – other characters were drawn more realistically in order to objectify them, emphasizing their 'otherness' from the reader." This principle applies to comic environments, as well. McCloud writes:

> In some comics, this split is more pronounced. The Belgian "Clear-Line" style of Herge's *Tintin* combines very iconic characters with unusually realistic backgrounds. This combination allows readers to mask themselves in a character and safely enter a sensually stimulating world.

McCloud makes it evident that above and beyond representational art, comic art is strategic. Symbolic, it serves a purpose. Comic art, it turns out, is very similar to the inflections described by rhetorician and literary critic Kenneth Burke in *The Philosophy of Literary Form*:

> They are not merely answers, they are *strategic* answers, *stylized* answers... These strategies size up the situations, name their structure and outstanding ingredients, and name them in a way that contains an attitude toward them.

Like other literary media, comics may often allude to outside plots or characters. But as McCloud noted, they have other assets as well. One of these is the look of the costumes. Many of the costumes in *Watchmen* don't seem to fit. This seems obvious enough, with some of the old Minutemen and Crimebusters, since they are from previous eras. But some of the other characters, such as Nite Owl, Ozymandias, the Comedian, or Rorschach, could be considered a bit pompous for their time, if not by their costume alone, then by the combination of their high-definition rendering super-imposed atop high-definition backgrounds.

Everything is very *real* in *Watchmen*. According to John Higgins, the creative team even debated how far away from Dr. Manhattan the color scheme should be affected by his pale blue aura and how the scene's lighting could color the wrappers of sugar cubes to which Rorschach keeps helping himself. This is a high-definition, highly detailed world. Considering this detail through McCloud's eyes, we might find the work as such: a high definition world tells us "this is the real world we are entering." Additionally, we find highly-detailed characters. If highly-detailed characters stand off from us, representing ideas rather than characters we can empathize with, it becomes apparent these characters *are indeed* caricatures. But for what?

The answer may lie farther down in the rabbit's hole that is the comic world. Let's take a minute to look at what is involved when we name a comic character. Here we again turn to Burke. Burke had a widely applied concept known as negative content. By naming something, we not only say what something is, we confine it to being only that. If I call a pair of scissors "scissors," we know they are not a pencil, paintbrush, or pillow. This principle becomes almost a governing rule in the comics world. Nowhere else are characters epitomized as thoroughly as they are in super-hero comics. To say that Barry Allen is the Flash is to say that he has only the powers of super-speed; it would be unfounded to expect him to have Superman's strength or X-Ray vision. Similarly, Spider-Man does not have the powers of Magneto; super-hero names are very rarely misnomers. Rather, we rely on them as rules, commands for what characters are and are not capable. Made in idealized fashion, they epitomize their respective abilities and namesakes. That is, if comic characters are identified by their respective abilities, so they also epitomize these to the point of conceptualizing the respective attribute.

Watchmen offers us caricatures, defined by their detail, and each specific name suggests what each caricature represents. The best example of this is Dr. Manhattan. I mentioned that we need to consider *Watchmen* as a situated text. But for *Watchmen*'s original readers, the Cold War's social unrest was everyday life. In this context, Jon Osterman's alias alludes to the Manhattan Project and, with it, the atomic power that still threatened very real nuclear annihilation. It's worth noting also that Dr. Manhattan gives the United States world sovereignty, or at least global security. This was also a benefit of atomic bombs in the initial period after World War II. Despite evidence of similar anti-Red feelings (as voiced by the editor of *The New Frontiersman*, for instance), we have a character whose nearly divine capabilities scare off the other countries from the arms race. In this way, Dr. Manhattan becomes not only a symbol for nuclear power but also shorthand for world conditions at the time.

In a world where world conflicts are dressed up in superhuman terms, we find the characters involved in a struggle similar to our own: the search for meaning in a life on the brink of nuclear precipice.

Throughout *Watchmen*, Moore and Gibbons present the idea that there is no point, no meaning to the world save whatever humans project upon it. We see this right from the start: on page four of Chapter I, Detective Steve Fine, talking about possible causes for Edward Blake's murder, says, "You know how it is... a lot of crazy things happen in a city this size. They don't all need motives." It's worth noting that this text is juxtaposed with a picture of the Comedian. Pondering nuclear fallout projections, President Nixon says, "It's like old naval battles. So much depends on a quirk of the wind. The wind's a force of nature, it's totally impartial... totally indifferent." In *Tales of the Black Freighter*, the narrator claims, "Fate had dealt its hand casually, despite my bitter protestations." When Rorschach recalls the events which transformed him, he says:

> Looked at sky through smoke heavy with human fat and God was not there. The cold, suffocating dark goes on forever, and we are alone. Live our lives, lack anything better to do. Devise reason later. Born from oblivion; bear children hell-bound as ourselves; go into oblivion. There is nothing else. Existence is random. Has no pattern save what we imagine after staring at it for too long. No meaning save what we choose to impose. This rudderless world is not shaped by vague, metaphysical forces.

In Chapter IX, Laurie Juspeczyk, while on Mars, tells Manhattan her earliest childhood memory. Reminiscing about a snow globe, she says, "I lifted it, starting a blizzard. I know it wasn't real snow, but I couldn't understand how it fell so slowly. I figured inside the ball was some different sort of time. Slow time... and inside there was only water." In her childish naiveté, Laurie wanted to believe there was something magical about the snow globe; she wanted to believe there was magic, or more, to life. As a jaded adult, she accepts there is nothing transcendent or miraculous about it.

Dr. Manhattan acts as a symbol for nuclear power and the world's condition. But in some instances, his perceived omnipotence makes him useful as a metaphor for human relations with the divine. From his vantage point on Mars at the end of Chapter IV, Jon Osterman wonders, "Which of us is responsible? Who makes the world? Perhaps the world is not made. Perhaps nothing is made. Perhaps it simply is, has been, will always be there... a clock without a craftsman." These are big words coming from the man who has "walked across the sun," and "seen events so tiny and so fast they hardly can be said to have occurred at all." Not least for his precognition, Dr. Manhattan can be taken as a figure of central authority and awareness. And his idea of the world being a clock without a craftsman is found over and over again throughout the series.

When the Comedian kills the Vietnamese woman at the war's end, Dr. Manhattan acts appalled. Blake retorts:

You watched me. You coulda changed the gun into steam or the bullets into Mercury or the bottles into snowflakes! You coulda teleported either of us to goddamn Australia... but you didn't lift a finger! You don't really give a damn about human beings. I've watched you.

Watchmen presents two approaches in response to its theme of a makerless world. The first is an approach of hopelessness. In the face of insurmountable odds, many of the heroes find themselves utterly inept to do any real good. Rorschach states, "This city is dying of rabies. Is the best I can do to wipe random flecks of foam from its lips?" Later, Veidt echoes this concern: "I fought only the symptoms," he says, "leaving the disease itself unchecked." Veidt admits to journalist Doug Roth, "I guess I've just reached a point where I've started to wonder whether all the grandstanding and fighting individual evils does any good for the world as a whole."

And yet the world's smartest man didn't come up with that idea; Edward Blake, the voice of hopelessness in the *Watchmen* world, brought it to him. At the Crimebusters meeting of 1966, Veidt says to Blake, "It doesn't require genius to see that America has problems that need tackling." Blake answers:

Damn straight. An' it takes a moron to think they're small enough for clowns like you guys to handle. What's goin' down in this world, you got no idea. Believe me. You people are a joke. You hear Moloch's back in town... You think that matters? You think that solves anything? ... It doesn't matter squat because inside thirty years the nukes are gonna be flyin' like maybugs... and then Ozzy here is gonna be the smartest man on the cinder.

Blake has the classic scope of man being overwhelmed by insurmountable odds. He sees the frivolous nature of human attempts to affect the world. Blake may be callous, but he is hardly obtuse. We see early on that, rough around the edges though he may be, Blake is a man who tries to find answers. Consider that even when he commits an act of rape, he verbalizes his justification as a response to an unasked question. "C'mon baby," he tells Sally Jupiter, "I know what you need. You gotta have some reason for wearin' an outfit like this." Even in his darkest moments, the Comedian tries to understand.

And Blake's understanding is vindicated by the other heroes. While talking to Laurie about getting in and out of the costumed hero business, Dan Dreiberg says, "But eventually[,] I realized the Comedian was right: it's all crap dressed up in a lot of flash and thunder." No less than Adrian Veidt describes himself and Blake as "intelligent men facing lunatic times."

In describing the other costumed heroes, Rorschach tells Dr. Long:

> No staying power. None of them. Except Comedian. Met him in 1966. Forceful personality. Didn't care if people liked him. Uncompromising. Admired that. Of us all, he understood most. About world. About people. About society and what's happening to it. Things everyone knows in gut. Things everyone too scared to face, too polite to talk about. He understood. Understood man's capacity for horrors and never quit. Saw the world's black belly and never surrendered.

Rorschach's notion that people understand reality in their gut but are too scared to face it offers a good measuring stick for contrasting the Comedian's perspective with others. Dr. Manhattan also makes note of this, saying:

> Blake is interesting. I have never met anyone so deliberately amoral. He suits the climate here: the madness, the pointless butchery... As I come to understand Vietnam and what it implies about the human condition, I also realize that few humans permit themselves such an understanding. Blake's different. He understands perfectly... and he doesn't care.

Blake is a version of joining what you can't beat, but with an ironic flavor. Rather than deny the insanity of life, he accentuates it. Comedians often take the things in life that bug us, whether big or small, and exaggerate them so we can understand, accept, and laugh at our foibles. They reverse the situation, amplifying things so we can see them better. Veidt says:

> I felt helpless against forces greater than any I'd anticipated. Too cowardly to confront life's black anxieties, I had life's black comedy explained to me by the Comedian himself back at the Crimebusters fiasco in '66. He discussed nuclear war's inevitability; described my future role as 'smartest guy on the cinder'... and opened my eyes. Only the best comedians accomplish that.

Veidt's shuttered his own eyes, refusing to see the world as it really is. As Rorschach claims, Veidt acknowledges horrors but won't face them. Then the Comedian makes a burning joke of the whole thing, and Ozymandias understands.

Consider two facts. We have a graphic novel full of characters who are caricatures, representing ideas rather than characters with which we identify. The graphic novel shows the true nature of something by poking fun at it, and one particular caricature among these, who is quite appropriately named, acts as the spokesman for comedy's cause. Combine these two, and I think you have the creators presenting themselves within the text. We have, in less than subtle whispers, an explanation for why *Watchmen* is a satire. Or a key to understanding the book through a manifestation of the makers' methods.

Watchmen provides an intricate, labyrinthine plot of a super-heroic epic. But as a situated text and a satire, *Watchmen* is a reflection of the world Moore and Gibbons lived in. Comic-book characters are merely the language they used to express it. This is as good as said outright in an excerpt from *Under the Hood*, in which Hollis Mason says, "All of us choosing to dress up in gaudy opera costumes and express the notion of good and evil in simple, childish terms, while over in Europe they were turning human beings into soap and lampshades."

The astute reader may notice that, although we have come to grips with the methods Moore and Gibbons employ, we haven't approached what their purpose might be. After all, the text is filled with passages building its theme of human inadequacy. Why express this idea if the creators feel it won't make a difference? So how's that joke go, again?

Moore and Gibbons give us two responses to their maker-less world. The first was one of embracing the insanity of our shortcomings as a joke. That was the method. The second approach is one of hope. It is our motive.

Embodied in Adrian Veidt, we find a rather humanist belief in humanity's ability to overcome. Consider the disparity between Blake's acceptance of our inability to change the world and the following excerpt from advertising copy for *The Veidt Method*, claiming the method, "if followed correctly can turn you into a superhuman, fully in charge of your own destiny. All that is required is the desire for perfection and the will to achieve it. No special equipment or hidden cash extras are necessary." Tongue-in-cheek though it may be, the idea is that you don't need to become Dr. Manhattan or own the expensive toys of Nite-Owl to change the world. And this idea is not found only here. At another point, Veidt claims, "You get to be a super-hero by believing in the hero within you and summoning him or her forth by an act of will. Believing in yourself and your own potential is the first step to realizing that potential."

Dan Dreiberg's dream corroborates this. Notice that, in his atomic nightmare sequence, his "skin" is not skin at all. It is a shell, containing the hero inside. Only when he dons his costume is he his real self. Earlier, Laurie notices the prototype for Dan's exoskeleton costume. "That sounds like the sort of costume that could really mess you up," she says. Dan replies, "Is there any other sort?" Dan has been wearing a mask of mild manners; suppressing his true self is killing him. Contrast that with a quote at the end of the chapter. Nite-Owl has shed his Dreiberg clothing, putting on his true form. He says, "I feel so confident[,] it's like I'm on fire. And all the mask killers, all the wars in the world, they're just cases – just problems to solve." This also references a much earlier statement made by Rorschach. Trying to make sense of Moloch's account of the Comedian's "last performance," Rorschach says, "So many questions. Never mind. Answers soon. Nothing is insoluble. Nothing is hopeless. Not while there's life."

It may also be that the point is not about achievement at all but about the process of simply doing. When Dr. Manhattan suggests the end of the Vietnam War must mean something to the Vietnamese, Blake replies: "Nah. Average Vietnamese don't give a damn who won. It means something to the dinks an' it means plenty to us... I mean, if we'd lost this war... I dunno. I think it might have driven us a little crazy, y' know? As a country. But thanks to you, we didn't, right?"

As the Comedian rightly notes, Dr. Manhattan won the war. Blake didn't, and neither did America. Yet the victory was important to Blake and his country. That Blake claims the war was won thanks to Dr. Manhattan reinforces the concept of a normal person's incapacity for impact; that Blake still fought the war shows us it's more about carrying on despite, or because of, the odds against us.

Speaking of an ad campaign for *Nostalgia* perfume at the end of Chapter X, Veidt observes, "In an era of stress and anxiety, when the present seems unstable and the future unlikely, the natural response is to retreat and withdraw from reality, taking recourse either in fantasies of the future or in modified visions of a half-imagined past." Perhaps in their attempt to escape by re-imagining, their use of the comic-book language showed Moore and Gibbons something revelatory about the very world they were trying to escape. Perhaps viewing the world as a satire revealed things the way the Comedian reveals things.

Rorschach is helpful here. Talking to Dr. Long, he says:

> Once a man has seen, he can never turn his back on it. Never pretend it doesn't exist. No matter who orders him to look the other way.
>
> We do not do this thing because it is permitted. We do it because we have to. We do it because we are compelled.

It's possible that, in an attempt to describe what they saw as irreparable damage, they were just lonely. Rorschach describes Blake as lonely: "He saw the cracks in society, saw the little men in masks trying to hold it together... He saw the true face of the twentieth century and chose to become a reflection, a

Eddie Blake confronts Edward Jacobi, the former Moloch. From Watchmen #2 (October 1986). Copyright © DC Comics.

parody of it. No one else saw the joke, that's why he was lonely." Maybe like the Comedian, they realized they were Pagliacci. Then, like Janey Slater talking to the *Nova Express,* they thought, "It's just such a relief to talk to somebody." As she says, some things can't be fixed once they're broken. It's a relief, she says, just to express that. This is the message of the Comedian.

However, there is one last angle from which to see this. The Comedian laughs at everything because he thinks the world can't be fixed. When he realizes it can be, he tells Moloch, "I don't get it. Somebody explain... somebody explain it to me." The irony is that the Comedian is the one who has been explaining things to us. He still will.

Ultimately, Blake causes his own end by motivating Veidt to action. Veidt confesses as much:

> I remember the charred map between my fingers; Nelson saying, "someone's got to save the world," his tremulous complaining voice... that's when I understood.
>
> Consoling Nelson, I left. Outside, Blake argued with Laurie and her mother. I swore to deny his kind their last black laugh at Earth's expense.

Veidt later tells Nite Owl and Rorschach, "Blake understood, too. He knew my plan would succeed, though its scale terrified him. That's why he told nobody. It was too big to discuss... but he understood. At the end, he understood." The larger point here is not that Blake knew Ozymandias was going to ruin the joke. The point is that he knew someone would end the comedy, and he knew it was the right thing to do. He didn't attempt to stop him.

In his final lesson, the Comedian's real punchline is that it's not about the joke. The joke helps us understand, but if we could do something about it, we should. Maybe that's why Moore and Gibbons kill the comedy right from the start.

Works Cited

Burke, Kenneth. *The Philosophy of Literary Form*. Berkeley: University of California Press, 1974.

Gibbons, Dave, Chip Kidd, and Mike Essle. *Watching the Watchmen*. London: Titan Books, 2008.

McCloud, Scott. *Understanding Comics: The Invisible Art*. New York: HarperPerennial, 1993.

Nothing Ever Ends: Structural Symmetries in *Watchmen*

by Jon Cormier

At the core of *Watchmen* is a text focusing on different points of view to create a fictional world that relates to our own. While there is an easy narrative to follow, the presentation of the narrative is done primarily through shifting perspectives and not necessarily limited to the characters' viewpoints. Just as the panels of a comic book create a viewpoint for the action of the page, the characters help create viewpoints for the reader to relate to and experience the world of *Watchmen*.

The different points of view help create meaning through their interaction in a manner similar to the way the interaction of text and art define comic books from other forms of art. The structure of the text is formally rigid (the nine-panel grid) and thematically symmetrical, reinforcing the shared relationship of the worldviews presented throughout the text. This process creates the idea of "fearful symmetry" as the driving metaphor for *Watchmen*.

The term "fearful symmetry" is taken from William Blake's poem *The Tyger*, and is used as the title for Rorschach's feature issue, but the fearful symmetry of the book is created primarily through the shifting point of view. The various costumed heroes are each trying to achieve a similar goal of peace and protection, but their actions all lead to some form of violence, aggression, and damage (psychological or physical). There is symmetrical imagery throughout the text – from Rorschach's mask to Dr. Manhattan's elemental symbol to Ozymandias's pyramid – but the symmetry of the text is not limited to iconography. There is also symmetry between the different points of view presented throughout the text, particularly between Rorschach and Ozymandias.

The "fearful" aspect of the metaphor is not merely the violent imagery and methods employed by some of the heroes, but in their detachment from their world and their own actions. The characters don't merely represent different points of view in *Watchmen*; they come to inhabit that viewpoint entirely. This detachment from their own actions (along with not realizing that the villains of the piece are acting from a similar point of view) is what defines the "fearful symmetry" of *Watchmen*. It becomes a bit scary for the reader when a piece of escapist fiction no longer maintains the clear distinctions between good and evil but muddies up the relationship into something closer to real life. That the costumed heroes and the world they inhabit so closely mirrors our own becomes something unfamiliar and fearful.

Cover Panel as a Window into the Fictional World

One of the groundbreaking aspects with which Moore and Gibbons presented to their audience was the plot of the comic beginning on the cover itself, rather than the first page proper. This departs from the norm of having a standalone cover present a dramatic scene splattered with hyperbolic text promising action and adventure – but ultimately offering only the illusion of change. Having the cover act as the first panel of the book helps place this comic within the reader's own world. This is not just a cover, but a window into a separate universe where the *Watchmen* characters exist, and like a window, it can act as a mirror when surrounded by darkness. This helps erase the first artificial barrier into every work of fiction – the cover keeping the text bound as a whole from the world around it. By opening a direct portal into the fictional world, Moore and Gibbons are, in essence, inviting the reader into a world that's an extension of his or her own. The old barrier that promised excitement and adventure, a break from the everyday, is not present in *Watchmen*.

Each cover panel is an extreme closeup of a detail which recedes into the background in the following panels. The initial view is always devoid of human presence, but as the wider scene is revealed, context is created for the initial detail by showing its relation to the people around it. The context is created only once the people and wider world are revealed. In the final chapter, the initial sequence is forgone to reveal only pages and pages of destruction; the comfort of the established slow build has been replaced by the shocking destruction of which the characters are capable.

While this is a very cinematic approach to revealing the setting (interestingly, the film version of *Watchmen* for the most part decided to forgo this approach), it is also an approach that parallels three of the main worldviews at conflict throughout the narrative. Rorschach deals with the world on a very immediate and close-up level; Ozymandias deals with the world at a lofty and removed distance; and Dr. Manhattan is capable of seeing both these views simultaneously, on levels both much closer and much further removed than either of these "human" characters.

This slow reveal helps situate the reader in the *Watchmen* world and is the first visual metaphor found in the work. The initial view reflects Rorschach's point of view and pulls out to reflect the view of Ozymandias. Dr. Manhattan views the world much like the reader, who examines the sequence as a whole or can focus attention on individual panels or details within each panel. Rorschach and Ozymandias could be represented by the bookend panels for the sequence and reveal their static limitations because of this, whereas Dr. Manhattan is malleable and beyond the rigid limitations of any single panel.

While the immediate and direct man-on-the-street perspective appears limited and the removed Olympian point of view appears wider-reaching or more open, ultimately both reveal rigidity and limitation, much as a single panel reveals its own limitations within the context of a comics page. On its own, a panel may contain more or less information than another panel; however, more information is always revealed through the relationship among multiple panels on a page. An individual panel allows sharper focus on individual moments. One shows the splash of blood on a smiley face pin; another shows the pin being washed away with the rest of the blood on the street.

Taking this flowing change in point of view to reflect the core conflict of Rorschach and Ozymandias shows how each is approaching the same problem from different points of the same angle. Rorschach takes to the street trying to save the city's residents from individuals, while Ozymandias distances himself from the city to see the larger picture of the global conflict in order to save humankind. Rorschach throws himself into direct conflict on a very intimate level; he breaks bones and inflicts violence on an individual level. Ozymandias destroys part of a city's population to save the rest of humanity from forces beyond their control. Each takes violent means to reach greater ends; each seeks to save people from themselves by imposing his own will upon them.

The worldviews of Rorschach and Ozymandias mirror one another in a fractal relationship, since they both try to save many by severely harming a few. The pattern is the same but the scale is different; just as the image on the cover is contained within the subsequent opening panels of each issue. And because of their limited and rigid points of view, neither sees how similar their actions and methods actually are.

Rorschach takes a surface read of the story's events, limiting his effectiveness to deal with someone working in the same manner on a larger scale. In some ways, it's funny that the trend for "grim 'n' gritty" comics following *Watchmen* stems in part from reading the comic with a similar filter to the one through which Rorschach sees the world. It's not just the immediate violence that makes Rorschach memorable; it's his relationship to Ozymandias's symmetrical undertakings and Rorschach's overall place in the larger plot and world of *Watchmen.* How many other comics suddenly abandoned thought balloons, sound effects, and heroism in hopes of emulating *Watchmen*? Yet how many of those same comics tried to create visual metaphors to reflect the plot and character relationships as *Watchmen* did?

Dr. Manhattan Inhabits the Space between Reader and Comic

There is only one character whose point of view can encompass a level of awareness close to that of the reader: Dr. Manhattan. His relationship to the world is one in constant flux and of a chronologically variable point of view. This is a character who can view the minute details of his world but exists at an intellectual distance so far removed from the human experience that he ultimately cannot remain on the planet. Each of the human heroes remain connected to the others by their shared sense of humanity and a need to protect some version of human interaction. Dr. Manhattan is in the process of realizing his own separation from humanity: not just humanity as a race but his own personal humanity and the world surrounding him.

Dr. Manhattan begins to reveal his distance from human context and behavior as he strips away clothing throughout the story's chronology. No longer confined to the limited viewpoint of "human," there is little reason for

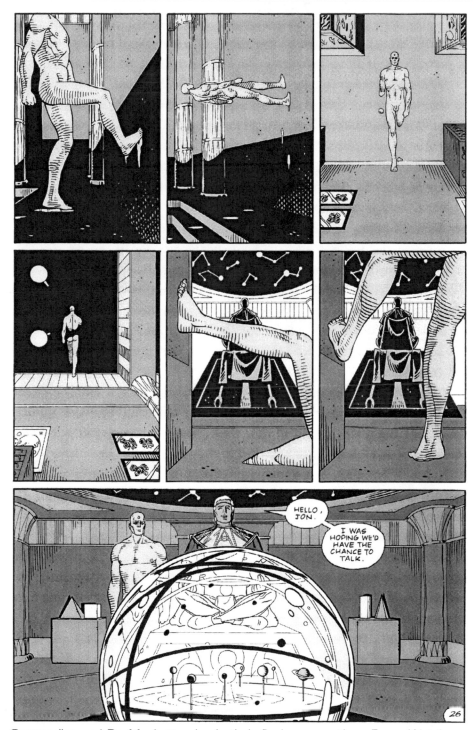

Ozymandias and Dr. Manhattan begin their final conversation. From *Watchmen* #12 (October 1987). Copyright © DC Comics.

him to constrain the rest of his existence in such a human manner. His naked blue form is both a comment on the history of the idealized human form used to portray costumed heroes and his own distance from human interaction.

Watchmen didn't totally erase the thought balloons so much as it reformatted them. Instead of a cotton-ball speech balloon floating above a character's head to display an internal monologue, that internal monologue is presented as some other form of communication; for example, Rorschach has his journal entries. Meanwhile, Dr. Manhattan has captions in the same shade of blue he inhabits. The human characters convey their inner thoughts to the audience through some form of in-story medium, like Rorschach's journal or the psychiatrist's notes. In contrast, Dr. Manhattan's thoughts come straight from his mind to the reader's eyes, without mediation. By having his thoughts relayed directly to the reader, Dr. Manhattan is established as a link between the other characters and the reader. He can approach his world the same way a reader approaches a comic book – rereading the whole story, focusing on particular details in a panel, skimming through, or reading just the dialogue. But Dr. Manhattan is still bound to the narrative. Only the reader exists beyond the narrative.

The nonlinear presentation of "Watchmaker," the chapter focusing on Jon Osterman and the creation of Dr. Manhattan, embodies how the creators manipulate the reader's point of view throughout the text, particularly at the climax. The comic-book form is limited to showing individual moments within each panel; however, these representative events don't need to be in chronological order. This non-chronological ordering not only presents Dr. Manhattan to the reader but allows the reader to experience the events of Dr. Manhattan's existence as near as possible to the character himself. The reader is limited by the linearity of the panel grid on the comic page, whereas Dr. Manhattan claims to be experiencing these moments simultaneously and indistinctly. It is his focus that must be adjusted to separate one moment from another, in the same way that a viewer's focus will apply meaning to a Rorschach blot. Dr. Manhattan seeing both past and present in a non-linear fashion is metaphorically like an analog watch, in that there is a cycle through time repeating itself. But for Dr. Manhattan, once the cycle reaches a new time, he doesn't see it as something new, and he is not bound by linear chronology. Dr. Manhattan can experience any point in time while regular humans will only ever witness distinct moments as part of a linear process. He continues to experience individual moments, whereas regular people will only have the memory of them.

Noticeable in this non-linear presentation are the interlaced images of cogs and other symmetrical designs in his creations. Much like the hydrogen symbol on his forehead, the ordered rotation of these items reflects how Dr. Manhattan views the world: as chaotically ordered systems and as a fractal pattern. This type of machination is also found in the workings of an analog pocket watch. The cogs themselves are symmetrical, but it is their points of contact that allow the system to have meaning. Without the contact points, the hands won't turn; Dr. Manhattan sees the points of contact and the hands moving. And in the end, it is the contacts amongst the human characters that convince Dr. Manhattan that humanity is worth saving. Only once his focus is shifted from the ordered symmetrical system to the points of contact does Dr. Manhattan return with Silk Spectre to Earth.

Just as the cogs in a watch interact, all the different aspects of this comic interact to create the story. Words and images work together to create the form, the characters interact with one another and the setting, the print publications at the back of the book interact with the reader to expand the fictional world, and most importantly, the writer and artist interact to put it all together so the reader can interact with the final product.

The watch-making imagery is also meant to be a play on the teleological argument of philosopher William Paley for the existence of God. The basic idea is that the complex nature of a system implies a creator, much like someone who has never seen a watch before would assume there had to be a watchmaker because of the complexity of its internal workings. It's no accident that the one person in the story interested in watch-making evolves into the one being who can see the metaphorical cogs of the physical world. Dr. Manhattan is capable of seeing the interaction of the atomic level just as he was capable of seeing the interaction of the clockwork when he was simply Jon Osterman. The symbol on his forehead is, again, something circular and symmetrical.

Fearful Symmetry through Shifting Points of View

The shifting points of view further reveal their fractal relationship in Rorschach's feature issue, appropriately titled "Fearful Symmetry." The issue is a symmetrical construction, with the last page reflecting the first, second last reflecting the second, until the pages meet in the middle spread depicting Ozymandias at a moment of violent confrontation. The layout, along with Rorschach's mask, makes the symmetrical part of the title seem obvious. Rorschach's unflinching and intimate approach to violence reflect the fearful part of the title. Taken together, the title's words remind the reader why Ozymandias is a central figure in this issue (literally as well as figuratively) and how his methods reflect those of Rorschach. Together, the actions of both heroes are fearful in their symmetry and symmetrical in their fearfulness.

The trouble with Rorschach's immediate viewpoint was that he could never see the bigger picture, even if it was constructed with the same materials he used; the trouble with Ozymandias's Olympian viewpoint is that it doesn't let him see the tiny splatter on the button. Ozymandias's view allows him only to see masses of people and not individual people performing individual actions. (This is foreshadowed at the end of his very first scene in the story, when we see him looking down on the distant city streets from his tower far above.) The most telling proof of this is the very end, when Ozymandias has failed to foresee the possibility of Rorschach's journal revealing the truth of the terrible actions that have created global peace. Rorschach becomes slightly less despicable only when he refuses to compromise, giving people the truth regardless of how ugly and brutal it may be. Rorschach never sees his own contradictory nature, given that what led him there was brutality towards the people he was trying to save.

Legacy Heroes: Different Generations, Different Points of View

The idea of fearful symmetry extends to the relationship between the legacy heroes; in particular, the two generations of Nite Owl. These characters meet to share their memories and ideals, thereby reinforcing their joint history and heroic identity. Their relationship becomes fearful when Hollis Mason is mistaken for the modern Nite Owl and killed out of vengeance and fear by the people he too once protected. This tragic death is caused by fear and stems from a misinterpreted symmetry between two different men.

The shared name of the Nite Owls is also a shared point of view between the two characters. Both Daniel and Hollis see their histories in a very similar manner. Both view their past with self-deprecating humor and appreciation, along with a humble regret at leaving it all behind. This humble regret is the seed inside Dan Dreiberg that grows to full bloom once Rorschach prods him to start investigating the Comedian's murder. Hollis presents his days as Nite Owl as a grand adventure, when speaking with Dan, but also presents the darker side to those happy-go-lucky times in his memoir *Under the Mask*. What both men share is a general dissatisfaction at their enforced retirement – by old age and by the law, both beyond their control.

Along with the dual Nite Owls, there are the mother and daughter versions of Silk Spectre; Sally Jupiter and Laurie Juspeczyk.   Here the inherited relationship between the two heroes is more direct and obvious.   The characters represent some core differences between the two generations of women (such as Sally Americanizing her Polish surname to Jupiter) and their differing approaches to men and sex. Sally is forced into a specific role by the men in her life, while Laurie sees the violence and pain behind the role her mother was forced into.   Laurie chooses her sexual partners, whereas her mother settles for a loveless marriage with a man who can provide for her daughter because, even as a costumed hero, she would not be accepted by society as a single mother. Even if she has fun with it, the original Silk Spectre is kept in a specific gender role by the men around her. Laurie's role, on the other hand, is never really questioned or defined by anyone other than herself or her mother. She's free to come and go as she pleases, and she chooses whether to be with Jon or with Daniel.

The only character to exist alongside both generations of Nite Owls and Silk Spectres is the Comedian.   With his real and secret identities remaining constant throughout the story, the Comedian becomes something of an anachronism.   Just as the different incarnations of Silk Spectre and Nite Owl reflect their respective eras, the Comedian reveals how maintaining a constant approach is not inherently good simply because it is unflagging. In this respect, he reflects the extreme positions taken by the other unique characters. Dr. Manhattan, Ozymandias, and Rorschach each take constant positions throughout the text just as the Comedian approaches everything with a violent detachment that treats humanity as a joke. The Comedian is a costumed, government-funded thug also seen attempting to rape a fellow hero – showing that bright costumes and being on the side of law do not always make someone into a paradigm the audience should emulate or relate to. Again, this is a conflicted character technically on the side of "right," but his methods make the end result feel less virtuous, no matter how necessary.

Even while portrayed as a pathologically violent thug, Blake's humanity is still revealed in his drunken confession to Moloch. Like the others, the Comedian is conflicted and has human failings. However, unlike the others who act heroically despite their failings, the Comedian never acts heroically. They act to find his murderer when it is unlikely that he would have done the same for them.

Under the Prose Pieces

In many ways, *Under the Hood* acts within the world of *Watchmen* as the comic does in our world; it removes some of the shine from the heroes and presents them as people dealing with difficult situations, exposing the weaknesses, humanity, brutality, and all the other behind-the-scene aspects of costumed heroes. Rather than present shining examples of heroism, these texts show aspects of the heroes that make them appear simultaneously less and more heroic: less heroic because they deal with the same mundane problems as regular people, but having the same fears and psychological issues, they become more heroic because they can overcome these same problems that keep regular people from achieving greatness. These are flawed individuals who still manage to defy their own limitations as well as those imposed from outside.

Under the Hood helps establish and frame the world in which the characters exist. The text pieces ending each chapter essentially help to widen the reader's perception of the *Watchmen* world as a more organic whole: a world that contains not just a costumed hero's memoirs but also pirate comics, scientific journals, publications aimed at liberal and reactionary worldviews, and the files of a psychiatrist. Readers get to know the fictional authors who created these pieces, while the pieces reveal more information about the world itself both from their content and the fact that they exist in the first place. The text pieces become both microscope and telescope through which readers experience the setting because each piece allows the reader to examine the wider culture within the story.

The fearful symmetry of the shifting point of view is also found in the other object used to parallel the plot within the *Watchmen* world. *Tales of the Black Freighter* serves as a parallel story to the main plot, reflecting the theme of the hero becoming the monsters he meant to fight, resulting in the hero alone destroying what he sought to protect. The *Black Freighter* sequences contain not only the fictional comic narrative but Bernard the newsstand owner's running monologue. Bernard's monologue parallels the comic within the comic, just as the *Black Freighter* comic parallels the comic book you're reading. This should lead the reader to wonder what the *Watchmen* comic itself is reflecting.

Parallel Plot Points Found through *The Tyger* and *Ozymandias*

The quotations that provide the title of each chapter are the final aspect extending this text into the real world. The quotations contain another fearful symmetry, in that the quotations relate to an issue's content by extending the metaphor into a real-world allusion. Each title creates meaning by linking the external reference to the issue's content by editing the quotation. While the shortened quotation divorces itself from the source, the wider implication of the quotations can be found in the source material. When the source of the quotations is explored, their true relationship to the plot and to the text becomes more profound.

The term "fearful symmetry" comes from the William Blake poem *The Tyger,* and while it is an appropriate description for Rorschach and his actions, the poem relates more to the ideas propelling the plot of *Watchmen* as a whole. The poem explores how a created world is capable of wonder through innocence but also fear through experience. The tiger of the poem is balanced by the lamb, just as the violence of Rorschach and Ozymandias is balanced by their goal of peace. In order to have the peaceful nature of the lamb, society must first confront the fear and violence of the tiger in order to know the difference. Peace and violence are intertwined and interrelated, just as each character in *Watchmen* is a mixture of success and failure. But more so, the worlds that Rorschach and Ozymandias wish to create are worlds of peace attained through violent means.

Percy Bysshe Shelley's poem *Ozymandias* is also apt in that the immediate action fits the edited wording about trembling at the sight of a man's mighty works. Yet taken in the context of the entire poem, this quote comes from an inscription on a dilapidated statue surrounded by a wasteland. No matter how powerful an individual or the realm he or she commands, both will be ruined by the passage of time. In *Watchmen*, the ambiguous ending allows for the possibility of the violently created peace to be undone through something as innocuous as a journal. The journal could be tossed to the side as the writing of a disturbed mind, or it could crumble the peaceful kingdom created by

Ozymandias.   While it is never revealed what destroyed the kingdom of
Ozymandias in Shelley's poem, it does point out the cyclical nature of human
endeavor in relation to creation and destruction. This is also reflected in the
cyclical nature at the core of Dr. Manhattan.

These documents extend the meaning of *Watchmen* into our real world.
The quotations relate the plot and characters to our own history and, in turn, to
our own state of affairs, at least as of 1986. If *Under the Hood* frames the world
of the characters in *Watchmen,* its fearfully symmetric counterpart would be
the *Watchmen* comic itself existing in our world. *Watchmen* reflects the real
world in how it manufactures meaning; it interprets our reality by not
presenting easy caricatures for the reader to identify. There is a violent peace,
the heroes are as violent as the villains, and the heroes are ultimately
responsible for the horrors witnessed. The costumed adventurers compromise
their ideals for expedient results, and in the end, the reader is presented merely
with protagonists, not heroes.

Conclusion: *Watchmen* as Window on the World

From shifting worldviews to the action being based around symmetrical
structures, *Watchmen* becomes a text exploring not just the form of super-hero
comics but the real world in scary detail. Just as each issue contains a visual
motif, such as the blood-splattered smiley face, each issue contains a quotation
which relates the fictional action to our own world. The final symmetrical
aspect is thus how the text itself reflects the real world. The plot is often
described as "realistic" because the conflicted nature of the protagonists
reflects the conflict and contradictions at the core of real people. The real
world is not as well-defined as old super-hero comics, and by blurring these
lines, *Watchmen* helps establish itself as a more realistic reflection of a world
without costumed heroes.

Costumed heroes were more heroic precisely because they couldn't exist in
the real world. The Golden Age heroes existed in a fictional world where good
and evil were clearly defined, and they reflected the social perceptions of the
world going through the Second World War. During the Cold War, the lines of
good and evil were less clearly delineated and as a comic from the end of that
era, *Watchmen* reflects the same social perception of a world unable to come
to grips with its own potential for destruction by forces never clearly defined.

And this symmetry is the most fearful of all.

58 Varieties: *Watchmen* and Revisionism

by Julian Darius

On page 10 of the first issue, one of the great secrets of *Watchmen* sits hiding in plain sight: a can of beans marked "58 Varieties."

It *should* be 57 – a reference to the real-life Heinz company, famous for its ketchup and advertised, at least in our world, with the slogan "57 Varieties." But here, for some reason, it's 58.

According to Heinz company lore, Henry John Heinz came up with "57 Varieties" while riding a train in New York City in 1896. Seeing a sign advertising "21 styles" of shoes for sale, Heinz sought to emulate the marketing ploy for his line of canned and bottled foods, including beans. The company actually sold more than 57 products, but Heinz chose 57 because five and seven were his and his wife's lucky numbers, respectively. He began employing the slogan "57 Varieties" in all his advertising.

It stuck, becoming part of Americana. Heinz soon erected a six-story tall, forty-foot long pickle bearing the words "57 Varieties" and illuminated by twelve hundred lights, which stood at the intersection of Fifth Avenue and 23rd Street in New York for nearly a decade. A popular urban legend claimed that you could get ketchup to pour from the bottle by tapping the "57," and *The New York Times* reported that this was the result of deliberate design by the Heinz

Dan Dreiberg returns home to an unexpected visitor from his past. From *Watchmen* #1 (September 1986). Copyright © DC Comics.

Company. Dogs of mixed breeds were sometimes called "Heinz 57s." The slogan is still used today, although it has somewhat faded from public consciousness.

There's no reason to think that Moore knew any of this when he wrote "58 Varieties" in his script for the first issue of *Watchmen*. All he was doing was suggesting that the world of the story wasn't exactly our own – that there were many subtle differences. It didn't hurt that Moore was playing with Americana, altering it just as he was forever altering the great American invention of the super-hero. It was just a minor flourish in one of Moore's scripts, notoriously filled with dense, detailed panel descriptions.

It's a detail worth appreciating, simply in this regard. Every panel is packed with similar details. In the hands of Dave Gibbons, every gesture reveals character and echoes recurring visual motifs, slowly imbuing them with meaning. It's altogether too easy to note *Watchmen*'s denseness: the way words undercut and comment ironically upon images, how symbols and visual patterns build and change, how a whole history and society is constructed and dissected through interwoven flashbacks, text pieces, and comics inserted into the text. Some of this world-building occurs on-panel: electric cars and plug-in power hydrants suggest advances in technology; Nostalgia perfume gives way to Millennium, signaling a change in the spirit of the age. But many on-panel cues, like "58 Varieties," are far more subtle.

A reader can take *Watchmen* from the shelf and open it to any random sequence and spend an hour in contemplation of a few pages, studying each word, each image, each panel composition, and the deep significance produced by the interplay between them. One could write an essay about any given page: its little details, how the panels work, how the page works within the chapter and within the whole, how each devastating thread of the overall work is echoed and undercut and layered on every single page. The whole is reflected in each detail, like in Laurie's snow globe or the bottle of Nostalgia perfume, spinning through the air on Mars.

Often, these details, just like "58 Varieties," suggest differences between this world and our own. A headline reads "Congress Approves Lunar Silos," suggesting that Dr. Manhattan's presence has preempted the international treaties that, in our world, prohibited nuclear weapons in space. Why negotiate such treaties when you have Dr. Manhattan? On page 25 of the first issue, a roast turkey with four legs is served at the restaurant where Dan and Laurie dine, apparently a sign that genetic engineering has become fairly commonplace in this timeline. And that's just the first issue, omitting more obvious cultural differences, from top-knot hairstyles to graffiti to the spherical design of the pipes Laurie and others smoke in place of cigarettes. But "58 Varieties" beats them all, because while most of the others more or less obviously stem from Dr. Manhattan's presence, there is no explanation for "58 Varieties."

Of course, "58 Varieties" can be read simply as a symbol for how this world is somehow slightly richer than our own. We have 57; they have 58 – close enough to be "realistic" from our point of view but with one notable addition: the super-hero.

This idea of adding just one element is actually central to the entire project of *Watchmen*, which can only be understood in the context of the overall agenda of revisionism, then being applied to the genre. That movement lacked any single manifesto, and it's nearly impossible to define. But it was inarguably focused on making the super-hero more artistically sophisticated and mature, which often meant injecting new levels of realism.

To some, the term only invoked a revision of what had come before: Moore had begun *Watchmen* as his take on the Charlton super-heroes, and detaching his story from those characters liberated him to push his revisions still further. For those who define revisionism narrowly, *Watchmen* is not a revisionist work since it featured new characters rather than revising old ones. Critics holding this view may prefer "deconstruction," borrowing the term from the popular theories of French philosopher Jacques Derrida. This alternate label emphasizes how the revisionist movement deconstructed the genre's old, clichéd formulas. And revisionism certainly *was* deconstructivist, but it wasn't interested in French theories. Instead, these comics-fans-cum-creators sought to aggressively revise not merely specific characters or old stories but the entire super-hero genre.

Not all of revisionism's many tendencies are embraced in any single work. For example, revisionism often carried its focus on making super-hero comics more sophisticated into the books' format and design. Thus, Frank Miller's *Dark Knight Returns* used minimalist covers, was printed on glossy paper, with longer stories, without advertising, and with an actual spine (in more ways than one). Earlier, Moore's "Marvelman" and "V for Vendetta" strips, in the U.K. magazine *Warrior,* employed lushly painted cover artwork that typically depicted its feature characters in symbolic images divorced from any actual story within. A year before *Watchmen,* a six-issue comic called *The One*, written and drawn by Rick Veitch and published by Marvel's imprint Epic Comics, had covers mimicking various icons and logos of corporate Americana: a Tide laundry detergent box, a can of Coca-Cola, a dollar bill, the face of a pocket calculator. *Watchmen* used simple, seemingly mundane images on its covers, letting them double as the story's first panel. *Watchmen* also signaled this concern with its text pieces, its better quality paper, its lack of advertising, its minimalistic back covers with dripping blood and a clock that both progressed over the series, and the inside covers that spelled out the title over all 12 issues. Later, Moore's revisionist *Batman: The Killing Joke* would follow many of these cues – using its inside front and back covers serving as the first and last panel, respectively.

This was more than sly packaging: it signaled that these projects, while ostensibly about super-heroes deemed silly and childish by mainstream adult culture, aspired to high art both inside and out. And there's a correlation here between the way *The One*'s covers appropriated Americana and what Moore and Gibbons did with the Heinz logo.

Revisionism also often played with narrative. Moore began this with "Marvelman" and "V for Vendetta," often telling each chapter in inventively different formats. Much of his *Swamp Thing* scripts for DC also did so; for instance, retelling the same brief vignette from the perspective of multiple observers over the course of one issue. Miller's *Dark Knight* juxtaposed panels frenetically, mixing flashbacks until they became their own iconography, jumping from scene to scene with abandon, and mixing shocking violence with TV panels to tell a story that rested on subtle references. *Dark Knight* built its page layouts around a grid of sixteen panels per page, as contrasted with the nine-panel grid used in *Watchmen*. *Watchmen* told its story with flashbacks and text pieces, but it also made recurring visual motifs, an alternate history of the comic book, depiction of a parallel-universe society, and tiny human moments as important as its few moments of super-heroic action.

Underlying this too was a desire to elevate super-hero comics to high art, to craft them with real literary weight. And what could be more literary than burying details in the backgrounds, like a Henry James novel in which every painfully meticulous description communicates character and culture? *Watchmen* did this one better by making those details textured, visual, and immediate – exploiting the visual strength of the comic-book form. Like, for example, that Heinz ketchup logo.

As many revisionists tried to lend super-heroes literary heft, they turned to high modernism with its demand that literature be realistic. We can argue over the artificiality of realism or which revisionist works embraced it in which ways, but there can be no doubt that revisionism sought (among other things) to inject the super-hero with unparalleled levels of realism. Moore's "Marvelman" did this exceptionally well, but it's here that *Watchmen* really excelled.

All of Moore's emphasis on the psychology of super-heroes in *Watchmen* wasn't about making Rorschach crazy for the sake of craziness, nor to inject new levels of violence into the super-hero. (If only Zach Snyder, for all his fidelity, had understood that!) It was about making the super-hero realistic, because the practice of taking to the streets in costume would, in the real world, attract people prone to psychopathology. Moreover, what the super-hero sees as he encounters real-life crime could easily cause a psychotic break. Policemen encounter scenes much like the one Rorschach recalls, and like Rorschach, they often lose their faith. But theirs is an occupation with its own formalized support network that costumed vigilantes lack. Unlike his subsequent imitators, Rorschach isn't two-dimensional: he *is* psychotic, but he also sees the world as it is – and this knowledge acts as a meme, infecting his prison psychologist, not to mention the reader.

Consider poor Dan Dreiberg, sexually impotent without the excitement of a rescue and the thrill of the costume. Or Dr. Manhattan, whose godlike powers distort his worldview until he feels wholly alienated from mankind; a direction in which DC would never allow Superman to evolve, however logical an outcome it may be. These aren't just great psychological portraits; they're ideological bombs, detonating the super-hero genre, forever exposing how unrealistic it had been up to that point.

At its highest, revisionism sought to place the super-hero into an utterly realistic world and show what might happen if he had to reckon with such an unfriendly environment. Or better yet, what *would* happen, managing to convey the sense of inevitability common to so much great literature.

One of the best discussions of comics revisionism ever published appears in the 1989 King Hell reissue of Rick Veitch's *The One*. The collected volume includes the transcript of a roundtable discussion by Neil Gaiman, Stephen Bissette, and Tom Veitch, focused solely on revisionism, for no better reason than that Rick Veitch cared about the overall revisionist movement and *The One*'s place in it. Far ahead of its time, it attempts to track the movement *as* a movement, including many often-ignored precursors and forgotten works.

In this discussion, Neil Gaiman offers the following insight on revisionism, key to understanding *Watchmen*:

> I think the point on the revisionist side of things is – science fiction. There are three classic tropes of science fiction: "what if," "if only," and "if this goes on." "If this goes on" is when you take a current trend, taking it to the ultimate, and see what you get. You say, look, people are driving dangerously on the freeways, so in twenty years time [...] You're not actually saying[,] "this is what's going to happen," you're just saying, "let's take something and extrapolate it." "What if" says, let's change one thing. What if aliens land? What if the sun goes out? [...] You keep everything else the same and watch how it gets distorted by the "what if"s.

Revisionism, for Gaiman, is about taking super-hero stories and putting them into the context of science-fiction "what if" stories, in which the world remains realistic except for a single development. Gaiman uses Moore's *Miracleman* (as "Marvelman" was retitled for U.S. publication after a threatened lawsuit by Marvel Comics) as an example: "The whole thing about *Miracleman* is that *Miracleman* [is] essentially about deformation, the way that reality is deformed, by one super-hero. What would it be like?" As Tom Veitch puts it, describing *Watchmen*: "Alan asks[,] if there really were costumed super-heroes, what would they be like in the real world? What would the government do about them?" The idea is to change one thing in an otherwise realistic world and see what happens.

Gaiman contrasts this with past super-hero stories in a way that not only illustrates what revisionism was rebelling against but is also instructive about how its realism operates:

> Now, in the world of Marvel Comics, because you want the world to be familiar to every reader picking it up, it doesn't matter that you have this giant green monster[,] who's going to come through San Diego in half an hour and destroy the city and bounce off, and it doesn't matter that Galactus is coming down... [laughter] Okay, let me try and give an example: a *Superman* story[,] written probably by Cary Bates in the early, say '74, '75. The NASA space program had pretty much just closed down. The plotline goes: a NASA scientist persuades Superman to take him to Mars briefly. While on Mars, he plants fake evidence of an alien life form on Mars, so that they can discover it[,] so that will give them the impetus to get the space program going. Now, hang on... you are talking about a universe in which you *know* there are aliens. There's one on Earth: he's

called Superman. There's J'onn J'onnz [Martian Manhunter]. Look, great spaceships come over every week, everybody knows there's life on other planets, so you aren't going to get the death of the space program. It doesn't make sense.

Gaiman does something far more interesting here than just trashing the silliness of old super-hero stories or even pointing out how unrealistic and inconsistent they are. Gaiman explains the *kind* of realism that revisionism sought to convey. Those silly stories, as he describes them, are ridiculous precisely *because* they are realistic: they had to keep the *world* realistic and recognizable to their young readers while simultaneously indulging super-heroes and other fantastic elements. Thus, any cities destroyed must be rebuilt in time to be destroyed again, sometimes in the next story. Those old stories were just as careful to put their finger on something and hold it in place, while letting the rest deform: it's just that they put their finger on the *world*, the *framework*, and not on the super-hero himself, who was allowed to play ridiculously *in* that framework. Revisionism would invert this formula, making the *super-hero* realistic by letting his world deform.

All this, of course, pertains to *Watchmen*. In Gaiman's words:

> *Watchmen* had two big "what if"s. One: what if in the 1940's, when the first batch of comics came out, people actually started dressing up and going out to fight crime inspired by the comics? And two: what if there was a real superhero, Dr. Manhattan, and what effect would he have on the world?

All of *Watchmen*'s cultural deformation – all the differences between *Watchmen*'s timeline and our own – are the consequences of these two "what if"s. Like any high modernist work, *Watchmen* was exceptionally controlled – as its nine-panel grid demonstrates. It inserts these two events into an otherwise realistic, recognizable world, then puts its thumb on them and watches the entire world deform until you get Tijuana Bibles about real-life super-heroines, comics about pirates instead of super-heroes, Dr. Manhattan in Vietnam, anti-hero riots, government regulation of super-heroes, a very one-sided Cold War, Nixon still in the White House, electric cars, genetically-altered animals, geodesic domes, and Nostalgia perfume.

Watchmen's parallel timeline is about this exploration of cultural deformation, itself a result of the text's revisionist agenda. This is what all those details, in the back of the issues and the background of the panels, are all about. In other words, *Watchmen* is just like our world, except that it has "58

Varieties" instead of 57. It has that one added element, and that makes all the difference.

Except that, as Gaiman and others are well aware, no single work really fulfills all of the requirements of this ideal. In its purest form, the highest revisionist text would make a single modification to a realistic world and then follow the threads of this "what if" with perfect logic and control. In narrative terms, there would be a single inciting incident, whether it occurs before the narrative begins or not, and everything else that departs from our own realistic world should be ripples from this initial condition, continuing until the world is transformed – like the so-called butterfly effect, in which a hurricane starts as a consequence of a butterfly flapping its wings half a world away. But revisionism was a movement, a loose association of concerns, with an agenda but not a detailed mission statement... and certainly not a prescription or a blueprint to follow.

This failure to control the unrealistic elements, to hold one's thumb firmly on the super-hero while the world transforms, applies to all the texts Gaiman mentions. Gaiman says that *Miracleman* is about a single super-hero deforming the world – except that he quickly adds the caveat that it's not a single super-hero but, "well, two or three super-heroes." There, one can argue that all the super-heroes were themselves the consequence of an earlier inciting incident – the crash of a single alien ship on earth – but other, problematically unrealistic elements are present as well.

In the case of *Watchmen*, the narrative cannot be understood without *two* such "what if"s. After Gaiman's makes this admission, Tom Veitch objects out that Dr. Manhattan isn't purely realistic either: he's "so pure he doesn't even wear clothes!" Even if we're inclined to forgive Dr. Manhattan's nudity as a logical psychological consequence of his awesome powers, we still have elements like the giant squid at the end – which we can forgive Zach Snyder for thinking a non-comics-reading audience simply wouldn't buy. *Watchmen* is a masterpiece but not a perfect one, and one can argue that it's a failure on its own terms, as an attempt at a high-realist super-hero story.

When Alan Moore briefly left super-hero comics shortly after *Watchmen*, it was partly because he felt he'd said all he wanted to say, taken the genre as far as he felt it could go; he was interested in telling human stories like that of Sally Juspeczyk and didn't need the super-hero construct to do that. When he returned to super-heroes in the 1990s, he had come to reject the entire idea of writing highly realist super-hero stories, preferring instead to embrace their unreality and sense of joy and wonder. It didn't help that people were copying *Watchmen* not by telling their own starkly innovative stories and pushing the medium but by telling copious humorless, violent stories of psychotic anti-heroes, mistaking *Watchmen*'s style for its substance, its skin for its heart.

We're welcome to think that Moore was right in his later assessment, remembering that even *Watchmen* had its unrealistic elements. As Moore has subsequently implied, it was a misguided attempt to take an unrealistic notion (the super-hero) and be really, really snooty about it – taking this fundamentally silly notion and crafting an otherwise realistic story around it. But we're also welcome to think that, for all his obvious talent, even Moore couldn't pull it off – unable to trump *Watchmen* or write another super-hero epic that more fully embraced realism, Moore simply retreated and ultimately rejected realism and revisionism altogether.

But then we get back to that ketchup logo and its "58 Varieties."

If we're inclined to read *Watchmen* as the failure of high revisionism, we can argue that Moore couldn't control his varieties; he couldn't stop at 58. In as much that logo serves as the symbol for how Moore has distorted society in *Watchmen* in subtle ways, we can argue that he didn't add one single ingredient into a realistic world at all. Instead, he inserted two... and we could argue, more than that. In other words, for all its apparent control, *Watchmen* is still an uncontrolled work – one that escaped its author.

As Moore has himself said, while he planned *Watchmen* in advance, not everything was intended from the start. Synchronicities kept building, and he found new resonances for the text's repeated symbols. He didn't know what every text piece would be; he thought one would be in the final issue, before Gibbons wanted to draw its opening sequence of splash pages. He's said that he didn't know that final scene with Sally Jupiter would play out the way it did until he wrote it and went with her kissing the Comedian's photo, because his gut said it felt right. *Watchmen*'s control is impressive, but what was originally unplanned – those varieties beyond 58 – is at least as interesting.

It's worth pointing out that "58 Varieties" also undercuts much of how revisionism has been misunderstood, based on its humorless imitators. Yes, the humor in *Watchmen* is typically gallows humor. And yes, it's intellectual, but it's not exactly dry. It's filled with passion. And it's filled, for all of its revisionism, with exactly the sort of wonder Moore loved in the comics of his youth – and which inspired him to return to super-heroes. What else can one call the glass clockwork mechanism created on Mars by Dr. Manhattan but a wonder? There's Veidt with his Antarctic base, with its beautiful, ironic greenhouse and its tachyon generators. There's Archie, the hovering Owlship. There's the joy of those stark visual motifs, those out-of-sequence Dr. Manhattan flashbacks, and that final revelation about Sally Jupiter, so touching and human and right, despite itself. The smiley face is, for all its punk irony and smeared blood, still smiling.

Because ultimately, 58 is *more* than 57. The super-hero may have been added to a realistic world, but it's a wondrous addition. And such fantasies, however older now and grown up, are still, like variety, the spice of life.

But there's one more thing to say about Heinz 58, before we stop beating this pale horse. There's a final take on that famous ketchup logo, one that helps unite the two disparate views above.

All the other examples of cultural deformation in *Watchmen* are consequences of what Gaiman identifies as *Watchmen*'s two inciting "what if" incidents. Everything else came from them. But Henry Heinz came up with "57 Varieties" in 1896, and that means the differences between our world and that of *Watchmen* go back at least as far.

We can well imagine Heinz on that train in New York City, seeing a sign advertising 21 styles of shoes for sale. Except that in *Watchmen*'s world, 8 was his lucky number rather than 7. And that, we're welcome to think, made all the difference. That may have been the inciting incident, generating a butterfly effect that altered culture just enough to make people take to the streets in the 1940s, imitating the early comics heroes and the pulps before them. And it may, through whatever chain of improbable, tiny consequences, have led to Jon Osterman entering that "intrinsic field subtractor" when he did, in 1959.

Then again, perhaps Heinz had a different lucky number because of an earlier incident in his life, itself the result of an earlier incident, riding a chain of causality back to some distant, unknowable flapping of wings.

In other words, Moore has built himself an out. In the text of *Watchmen* itself. In the very first issue. Whether he intended it or not, it's there. And it's not too much to say that Moore may have had this idea (at least loosely) in mind: that there was some inciting incident long before either of his two big "what if"s that set everything in motion.

This means, should we want, we can have our cake and eat it too. *Watchmen* is an arch-revisionist work full of unparalleled realism and control – so much so that it encodes in a single, apparently unimportant object sitting on a table the notion that these distortions in the timeline go back at least to 1896, if not further. But it also means that (because we can always postulate an earlier "what if" to cause a butterfly effect) we can revel in all of *Watchmen*'s wonders, fully justified that their lack of realism has an unseen origin – that like biological life itself, all this wonder evolved from something horribly mundane and impossibly remote.

Don't believe that all this could lay implicit in a single ketchup logo? Forget that *Watchmen* is about causality. Forget that *Watchmen* is full of such apparently unexplored detail. Forget that the emblem of its first issue and its first panel and arguably its whole is the blood smear on the smiley face, which Rorschach (in the same scene with the Heinz can of beans) calls "human bean juice."

How does *Watchmen* end? What's its final image? That's not blood the second time around: it's really ketchup, dashed across a knowing smile. Yes, *Watchmen* ends with ketchup, conveying some deep and ambiguous meaning.

You don't have to believe me. I leave it entirely in your hands.

Bringing Light to the World: *Watchmen* from Hiroshima to Manhattan

by Peter Sanderson

In the second issue of *Watchmen*, the vigilante Rorschach walks past a strip club on Manhattan's 42nd Street. A sign outside advertises an act called "Enola Gay and the Little Boys." Readers with a knowledge of history should be taken aback: the Enola Gay was the name of the B-29 Superfortress bomber that dropped the atomic bomb, code-named Little Boy, on the Japanese city of Hiroshima near the close of World War II.

But what is this reference doing in *Watchmen* – a series set in an alternate history, primarily in 1985, some 40 years after the end of that war? The careful reader will find many references to the bombing of Hiroshima and the subsequent bombing of Nagasaki throughout *Watchmen*. They are hardly accidental.

One of the principal subjects of *Watchmen* is America itself, from the late 1930s to 1985, a time span in which the super-hero genre originated and evolved in comic books. The history of the super-hero genre coincides with the United States's development into a national superpower, beginning with its transition from isolationist nation to a major combatant in World War II. In

Watchmen, Alan Moore and Dave Gibbons portray super-heroes as archetypal figures of America and link these fictional heroes to real events in American history. Through this device, Moore and Gibbons investigate and question American society, politics, and morality. As such, Hiroshima and Nagasaki are a recurring motif in *Watchmen*.

Hiroshima in History

Following the end of World War II in Europe, the United States, United Kingdom, and China issued the Potsdam Declaration on 26 July 1945, demanding unconditional surrender by Japan and warning that "the alternative for Japan is prompt and utter destruction." Although the Japanese emperor Hirohito and a faction of his government wanted to surrender, the Japanese military was insistent on fighting on.

During the war, the United States developed the first atom bombs through its secret Manhattan Project. President Harry S. Truman ordered that an atom bomb be dropped on the city of Hiroshima. The Enola Gay dropped the bomb, dubbed "Little Boy," at 8:15 AM on the morning of 6 August 1945.

According to the U.S. Department of Energy, "a huge explosion lit the morning sky as Little Boy detonated 1,900 feet above the city." Colonel Paul Tibbets, pilot of the *Enola Gay*, recalled that "the city was hidden by that awful cloud... boiling up, mushrooming, terrible[,] and incredibly tall." The Department of Energy notes that "those closest to the explosion died instantly, their bodies turned to black char." The intense light and heat of the explosion preceded the shockwave of the atomic blast: "The white light acted as a giant flashbulb, burning the dark patterns of clothing onto skin and the shadows of bodies onto walls. Survivors outdoors close to the blast generally describe a literally blinding light combined with a sudden and overwhelming wave of heat." Many were killed within minutes of the explosion; many more died in the resulting firestorm. Radiation killed still more, either within weeks or months from radiation sickness or years later from cancer.

Three days later, at 11:01 AM on 9 August 1945, the B-29 Superfortress Bockscar dropped another atom bomb, "Fat Man," on the city of Nagasaki, greatly adding to the death toll.

Less than 11 hours before the bombing of Nagasaki, the Soviet Union had entered the war against Japan. As a result of this combination of factors, the faction favoring peace ultimately prevailed, and the Emperor of Japan surrendered to the Allies on 15 August 1945 via a prerecorded radio broadcast.

From 1945 to the present, the American public has generally seemed to accept the bombing of Hiroshima and Nagasaki as necessary for ending World War II. Although Truman was deeply unpopular for various reasons when he left office, his reputation has improved considerably over succeeding decades. Nonetheless, Truman's decision to use the atom bomb has remained controversial. Even Truman's successor, Dwight Eisenhower, disagreed with the decision to drop the bombs. The 1946 United States Strategic Bombing Survey asserted that the atomic bombing of the two cities was unnecessary for ending the war. In 1963, the District Court of Tokyo declared the bombings to be war crimes. In 1967, Noam Chomsky asked,

> To what extent are the British or American people responsible for the vicious terror bombings of civilians, perfected as a technique of warfare by the Western democracies and reaching their culmination in Hiroshima and Nagasaki, surely among the most unspeakable crimes in history?

The bombing of Hiroshima and Nagasaki ended the Second World War, but it was soon followed by the Cold War. Once the United States and the Soviet Union had nuclear arsenals, tensions between the two could have led to nuclear war. Indeed, the two nations came to the brink of World War III during the Cuban missile crisis of 1962. *Watchmen* does not mention that crisis; perhaps, due to the presence of Dr. Manhattan, it never happened in that history. But by 1985, the United States and Soviet Union are moving towards a worldwide nuclear war.

Images of Armageddon

Watchmen falls into a tradition of stories, sometimes called apocalyptic or eschatological, about the potential end of the world. As early as panel three on the first page of Chapter I, we see Rorschach in his civilian identity carrying a sign reading "The End is Nigh." The bombing of Hiroshima, introducing the use of atomic weaponry, was the first link in a chain of events that could culminate in the end of the world through nuclear war.

The cover of Chapter III shows a fallout shelter sign with the international black-on-yellow trefoil symbol indicating dangerous radiation. The cropping of the image and the smoke drifting over it means that the only unobstructed letters on the sign read "ALL HEL." The first panel of the story opens with the narration of the unnamed mariner from *Tales of the Black Freighter*, referring to "the hell-bound ship's black sails against the yellow Indies sky." Thus, the black-on-yellow fallout shelter sign becomes the counterpart of the Black Freighter. The same panel contains a comment by the news vendor, who says, "We oughta nuke Russia, and let God sort it out." In the next panel he adds, "I see the signs," which may be Moore's ironic allusion back to the fallout shelter sign.

In panel three, we see the sign again when the *Black Freighter* narrator reports that the Freighter's demonic crew "called out, 'More blood! More blood!'" – against which is juxtaposed copy of *The New Frontiersman* with a cover story about a "missing writer." This is Max Shea, author of this very *Black Freighter* story, who has also played a role in creating the creature that Adrian Veidt will use to kill half the population of New York. This same panel closes with the off-panel news vendor declaring, "We oughta nuke 'em till they glow!"

This sequence of panels demonstrates Moore and Gibbons's method of linking visual and verbal imagery to their themes and demonstrates how fully the theme of nuclear war infuses the series. It also subtly establishes an image that will recur in *Watchmen*: the "glow" reminiscent of the brilliant light of the detonation at Hiroshima.

In the next-to-last panel of page four, Bernard the news vendor is startled by the arrival of Walter Kovacs, looking fearsome and ominous in the page's final panel. Cast into shadow by a setting sun, he carries his sign, "The End is Nigh," and asks, "Is it here yet?" He is literally referring to *The New Frontiersman*, but in context, he could also be referring to the end of the world. Indeed, Bernard asks him on page five, "How's the enna the world comin' along?" Again, significantly, we see the *New Frontiersman* cover featuring Max Shea, who will help bring about the end of the world, at least for half of New York.

Later, when Dan Dreiberg talks with a distraught Laurie Jupiter, he remarks, "Whatever's bothering you, it's not the end of the world, right?" But Laurie has left her relationship with Dr. Manhattan, who served as a one-man deterrent to nuclear attack by the Soviet Union. When he leaves Earth at this issue's end, that deterrent is gone, so it is indeed "the end of the world" that bothers Laurie.

On page 11, we see posters for the rock group "Pale Horse." The name refers to a line from Revelation 6:8 describing the Fourth Horseman of the Apocalypse: "And I looked, and behold a pale horse: and his name that sat on him was Death, and Hell followed with him." Popular culture in the world of

Watchmen is increasingly preoccupied with death and prophecies of the end of the world.

Through Veidt's scheming, Dr. Manhattan is unjustly accused of inducing cancer in various people, just as many survivors of atomic blasts develop forms of cancer due to radiation exposure, sometimes more than 20 years later.

The radiation symbol seen on the fallout shelter is placed on the door of Dr. Manhattan's quarters when they are quarantined for possible radioactive contamination. By the end of the issue, that same symbol appears repeatedly on a map in the President's war room to mark areas of America that would be affected by fallout in a Soviet nuclear attack.

The Bomb in Human Form

Dr. Manhattan is, in effect, the power of nuclear energy in human form. His coming represents the Atomic Age in world history. Hiroshima explicitly plays a part in the chapter titled "Watchmaker," recounting how the human scientist Jonathan Osterman was transformed into the godlike Dr. Manhattan.

In 1945, the teenage Jon Osterman practices watch repair when his father shows him a copy of the *New York Times* bearing a headline about the dropping of the atom bomb. The elder Osterman says,

> Forget pocket watches! Have you seen the news? They dropped the atomic bomb on Japan! A whole city, gone! Ach! These are no times for a repairer of watches... This changes everything! There will be more bombs. They are the future. Shall my son follow me into an obsolete trade?

The old watchmaker continues, "This atomic science... this is what the world will need! Not pocket watches!" The elder Osterman explains, "Professor Einstein says that time differs from place to place. Can you imagine? If time is not true, what purpose have watchmakers, hein?" And he drops the watch mechanisms Jon was working on off a fire escape.

Jon's father overreacts in that, of course, people will still need to tell time in their everyday lives, but his reference to Einstein is significant. Einstein not only devised the formula that made the atomic bomb possible but also propounded the theory of relativity, which states that time moves at different rates, depending on the reference frame of the observer.

Although he cannot articulate it, the watch represents to Jon's father the Newtonian vision of the universe, characterized by an order that was relatively simple to grasp. "My father admired the sky for its precision," says his son. The atom bomb represents the new Einsteinian vision of the cosmos, in which not even time has an absolute, constant value. Indeed, once Jon becomes Dr. Manhattan, he perceives time differently than normal humans, seeing his own past, present, and future as if they were simultaneous. The storytelling structure of "Watchmaker," with its flashbacks and flash-forwards, seeks to capture something of the way that Dr. Manhattan experiences time.

Moreover, Jon's father seems to foresee that the destruction of Hiroshima will lead to the age of superpower nations with nuclear arsenals: "There will be more bombs. They are the future." Perhaps he means that fixing pocket watches is meaningless when the safety of the world will be at stake. Perhaps he urges Jon to become a physicist because he thinks this will be the means of understanding and perhaps controlling a universe that now seems more complex and dangerous. This is a future characterized by bombs, characterized not by creation but by destruction – potentially on a planet-wide scale.

Despite his father's claim of obsolescence, Jon as an adult nuclear physicist continues to think like a watchmaker. As he and co-worker Janey Slater fall in love, we see Jon repairing a watch, and Dr. Manhattan recalls, "Events mesh together with soft precision." When a "fat man" steps on Janey's watch, breaking it, Jon promises to fix it. Is it a coincidence that "Fat Man" was the code name of the atom bomb dropped on Nagasaki?

Trapped within the intrinsic field subtractor chamber, awaiting his own death, Jon is looking at the repaired watch when the chamber activates. "The light... the light is taking me to pieces." Gibbons depicts Jon as a skeleton silhouetted against the bright light of the radiation, evoking the shadows of victims on the walls at Hiroshima, an image we will encounter again.

When Osterman recreates his body, Moore and Gibbons intercut the now-familiar panel showing a hand (presumably Jon's) working with watch parts, and they have Jon saying in narration, "Really, it's just a question of reassembling the components in the correct sequence." Jon has become a godlike being who imposes order on reality – no longer a literal repairer of watches but a figurative "watchmaker" who operates on a higher level, with the power to restructure reality. Moore thus presumably refers to the celebrated analogy between God and a watchmaker, most famously set forth by the British philosopher William Paley in his 1802 book *Natural Theology*. In his opening page, Paley establishes the analogy between the universe and a watch; on finding a watch, Paley writes,

The inference, we think, is inevitable, that the watch must have had a maker: that there must have existed, at some time, and at some place or other, an artificer or artificers who formed it for the purpose which we find it actually to answer; who comprehended its construction, and designed its use.

Dr. Manhattan recalls that according to his government supervisors, "the name has been chosen for the ominous associations it will raise in America's enemies" – a reference to the real life Manhattan Project, which developed the atomic bomb.

The government provides Dr. Manhattan with an insignia based on the international symbol for the atom. (The symbol is used as the logo of the U.S. Atomic Energy Commission; it also serves as the emblem of Dr. Manhattan's fictional inspiration, the Charlton super-hero Captain Atom.) But he observes that "a hydrogen atom would be more appropriate," and he in effect tattoos a hydrogen atom symbol directly onto his forehead. This likens Dr. Manhattan to a living hydrogen bomb.

Osterman continues, "They're shaping me into something gaudy and lethal." Moore and Gibbons then insert a panel showing the young Jon and his father with the *New York Times* headline about the bombing of Hiroshima, making it plain that the U.S. government seeks to use Dr. Manhattan as a living version of the atomic weapon that devastated Hiroshima.

Arguably, Dr. Manhattan also embodies postwar America as a superpower, a status it possesses in large part due to its nuclear arsenal. A flashback to the Vietnam War shows Dr. Manhattan as a literal colossus, dominating the landscape, overpowering opposing forces. He recalls that "often [the Viet Cong] ask to surrender to me personally, their terror of me balanced by an almost religious awe. I am reminded of how the Japanese were reported to have viewed the atomic bomb, after Hiroshima." This not only underlines the identification of Dr. Manhattan with the atomic bomb but explicitly connects him to Hiroshima. Moore may here be suggesting that the Vietnam War was an extension of the bombing of Hiroshima: America using superior might to overwhelm Asian people.

Several pages later, Dr. Manhattan recalls, "It's August 1985. I'm walking through Grand Central Station with Laurie. We stop at the newsstand and buy a copy of *Time* magazine, commemorating Hiroshima Week." He observes that "on the cover there is a damaged pocket-watch stopped by the instant of the blast, face cracked..."

The shadows of Hiroshima loom large across history.   From *Watchmen* #4 [December 1986]. Copyright © DC Comics.

Here is another indication of the effect of Hiroshima on American consciousness in *Watchmen*'s world: there is a "Hiroshima Week," memorializing the event.   (Presumably, Moore chose *Time* rather than *Newsweek* since time is such an important theme in this issue of *Watchmen*.) The cover may reinforce the contention of Jon's father that Hiroshima made watch repair obsolete.   The bombing stopped the watch on the cover, symbolically ending the reign of Newtonian physics.   Perhaps the shattered watch is yet another omen of the end of the world: a nuclear war would end the history of human civilization. The shattered watch may also be a reminder of Janey's broken watch, once again linking Hiroshima with Dr. Manhattan's origin.

(In our world, the cover of *Time* magazine from 29 July 1985, commemorating the fortieth anniversary of Hiroshima that week, was a photograph of the nuclear mushroom cloud erupting over the city, taken by a Japanese photographer on the ground. The photo was accompanied by a quote from the co-pilot of the Enola Gay: "My God, what have we done?" Interestingly, in our world, that issue of *Time* also includes an interview with former President Richard Nixon, discussing atomic warfare.)

The panel with the *Time* cover is followed by a panel repeating the image of Janey handing the beer to Jon – the moment in which their relationship began. Is this because Jon's relationship with Janey is also shattered beyond repair?

In the issue's final pages, Dr. Manhattan wonders if the universe is "a clock without a craftsman," if there is no "watchmaker" God who created it. Through the juxtaposition of these words and the imagery of the closing page, the clock parts that Jon Osterman's father dropped off the fire escape are linked both to the atomic bombs falling on Hiroshima and Nagasaki and to the meteor shower in the last panel.

"Watchmaker" is followed by the text feature "Dr. Manhattan: Super-Powers and the Superpowers," supposedly written by Professor Milton Glass. The title makes a connection between the superhuman Dr. Manhattan and the United States as a "superpower" nation. Glass notes the irony that "man, when preparing for bloody war, will orate loudly and most eloquently in the name of peace." Readers should remember this when, in the later issues, Veidt orates eloquently about peace as he carries out the Manhattan massacre.

Making indirect reference to Hiroshima, Glass writes that "the Second World War – we were told – was The War to End Wars. The development of the atomic bomb is the Weapon to End Wars. And yet wars continue." The Hiroshima bomb led to a nuclear arms race among the great powers. Glass goes on, "The wars to end wars, the weapons to end wars, these things have failed us. Now we have a man to end wars." Dr. Manhattan, America's living nuclear deterrent, thus becomes the latest version of what the Hiroshima bomb was supposed to be. "By placing our superhuman benefactor in the position of a walking nuclear deterrent, it is assumed we have finally guaranteed lasting peace on Earth." Instead, Glass concludes, "I do not believe we have made a man to end war, I believe we have made a man to end worlds." Dr. Manhattan's existence makes the Soviet Union feel sufficiently threatened to launch an all-out nuclear assault, with too many missiles for even Dr. Manhattan to stop.

Shadows of Love and Death

On page 11 of Chapter V, Rorschach sees a group of boys spray paint an image of two silhouetted figures in a doorway, a "man and woman, possibly indulging in sexual foreplay." Rorschach doesn't like it: "It makes doorway look haunted." Rorschach's reaction may reflect his own dysfunctional attitudes towards sexuality; in the previous panel, he refers to his prostitute mother. But perhaps he feels haunted because this is another reference to the ghostly silhouette figures of dead victims on the walls of Hiroshima. The fact that youths spray paint similar images again shows the grip of the Hiroshima bombing on popular culture in the world of *Watchmen*. (In the page's last panel, Rorschach has created a "Rorschach blot" on a menu while we see another spray-painted pair of silhouettes in the background, suggesting that he interprets the silhouettes as if they were part of a Rorschach test – a key to his own psyche.)

But why the silhouettes of a pair of lovers? This has an interesting ambiguity. It could mean that the destructive force of atomic weaponry like the Hiroshima bomb puts an end to love, sex, and life. Hence, it could be an omen of the imminent possible nuclear war. Atop page 18, Rorschach holds up a note, supposedly from Moloch, as we see the silhouetted lovers in the background. Are the lovers an omen of death? Rorschach will soon find Moloch murdered. But the silhouetted lovers could also mean that love and the life force transcend the death and destruction of war: the lovers may be killed, but this image of their love survives.

In the following chapter, prison psychiatrist Dr. Malcolm Long administers a Rorschach inkblot test to the incarcerated Walter Kovacs.   Interestingly, Gibbons portrays Long and Kovacs as a couple cast nearly in silhouette atop pages two and 16, perhaps suggesting the intimate bond between doctor and patient. One of the Rorschach blots reminds Kovacs of the silhouetted figures of his mother and one of her clients having intercourse. The sequence ends with the shadows of Kovacs' mother inflicting pain on her son. Though the boys with the spray paint may intend their figures of silhouetted lovers as an image of love, one can see why Rorschach interprets them differently.

Later, Gibbons shows Dr. Long in an affectionate embrace with his wife, and they become silhouette figures in one panel.   But as Long becomes more obsessed with Rorschach's case, he grows more distant from his wife, who appears as a shadow in an angry stance on page 13.

Pointedly, Dr. Long mentions that "On Seventh Avenue, someone had spray painted silhouette figures on the wall.   It reminded me of the people disintegrated at Hiroshima, leaving only their indelible shadows." As Long and his wife continue to move apart, Long says that, "on 7th Avenue, the Hiroshima lovers were still inadequately trying to console one another." The silhouettes have become a Rorschach test for Long, who interprets them according to events in his own relationship with his wife.

The text feature for Chapter VI includes an essay written by Kovacs at age 11, in which he states, "I like President Truman, the way Dad would have wanted me to. He dropped the atomic bomb on Japan and saved millions of lives because if he hadn't of, then there would have been a lot more war than there was and more people would have been killed. I think it was a good thing to drop the atomic bomb on Japan."

This was indeed the government's rationale for using atomic bombs on Hiroshima and Nagasaki. The alternative, an invasion of Japan, would have been extraordinarily costly in both American and Japanese lives. By putting this defense of the bombing into the mouth of a disturbed, 11-year-old boy, Moore suggests that such a rationale is the result of naive, immature thinking. Moore also seems to suggest this kind of thinking can lead to fanaticism, as it does with Kovacs as he becomes the adult Rorschach, who rationalizes the use of torture and murder in his war on crime.

Trial by Atomic Fire

At the start of Chapter VII, Laurie accidentally activates the flame thrower on Dan's Owlship, creating a blaze that Dan has to extinguish. Fire becomes a major motif of this chapter, including the fire from a nuclear blast.

12 pages in, Laurie worries, "Has the big countdown already started?" The imminence of World War III reminds Dan of Hiroshima: "During Hiroshima Week, I read an article in *Time* Magazine, with pictures: kids' bodies, skin burned black." Soon afterwards, Dan tries unsuccessfully to have sex with Laurie, while on the television Adrian Veidt masterfully performs acrobatics, followed by an appearance of rock musician Red D'eath of Pale Horse. Veidt acts (by himself) while Dan cannot, and death follows in Veidt's wake.

Dan has a dream in which he and Laurie embrace, while a nuclear explosion erupts behind them in a mushroom cloud. The bright light of the detonation engulfs them, transforming them into silhouetted skeletons as they kiss. Like the Japanese dead who left their shadows on the wall, Dan and Laurie become victims of a new, far greater version of the Hiroshima bombing: the anticipated nuclear war.

Dan later describes the dream to Laurie, referring to the blast as if it were fire: "We – we were kissing, and then this nuclear bomb, it just... we burned up. We were gone, everything was gone..." He confesses, "It's the war, the feeling that it's unavoidable. It makes me feels so powerless... so impotent" – both as a former super-hero and as a potential lover. He speaks of "this anxiety, this terror bearing down."

But Dan overcomes his anxiety and impotence when he and Laurie resume their super-heroic guises as Nite Owl and Silk Spectre and head out in his flying Owlship. Together, they rescue people from a burning building, and subsequently, they successfully make love aboard the Owlship.

Laurie attributes their sexual success to the "costumes." But there is more to it: Dan has overcome his impotence not only as a lover but as a hero – as a man capable of making a difference in the world for the better. He and Laurie have performed a heroic deed. Whereas earlier they spoke of "kids" who were "burned" in the Hiroshima bombing, now they have rescued children from burning in a fire. Similarly, Dan had described how, in his dream, he and Laurie were "burned up" by the nuclear bomb, but now they have successfully survived the fire from which they rescued people.

Newly confident of their ability to fight back against the world's dangers, Dan and Laurie are able to make love despite their awareness of being on the brink of World War III. While doing so, they trigger the flame thrower, and the jet of fire becomes an obvious sexual symbol. Rather than being consumed by flame, now they create flame through their passion. (Veidt later observes that there is "an erotic undercurrent not uncommon in times of war.")

Instead of fearing the fire representing nuclear destruction, Dan has become a master of metaphorical fire himself. One could argue that the nuclear explosion in Dan's dream was also a visual metaphor for the sexual emotion between himself and Laurie, which he also seemed to fear. Now, however, Dan tells Laurie, "I feel so confident, it's like I'm on fire, and all the mask killers, all the wars in the world, they're just cases, problems to solve."

The chapter concludes with a quotation from *Job*: "I am a brother to dragons, and a companion to owls. My skin is black upon me, and my bones are burned with heat." Dan has taken the owl as his motif, and he now is also like a dragon who breathes flame rather than fearing it. At the beginning of the chapter, Dan spoke with horror of children whose skin was burned black by radiation at Hiroshima, but now Dan has undergone a trial by fire in rescuing other children. Metaphorically, his skin is burned "black upon me" and his bones are "burned with heat." But rather than killing him, the "fire" has made him stronger, arguably like Job.

New York as New Hiroshima

Max Shea, author of *The Black Freighter*, and artist Hira Manish participate in creating Veidt's genetically engineered monster, thinking they are working on a movie and unaware of Veidt's true plans. They leave their island base aboard a ship bearing the logo of Veidt's Pyramid Industries: a triangle in a circle that should remind readers of the radiation warning sign. Shea and Manish are about to have sex when Shea discovers a bomb. He embraces her, and their shadows are cast on the wall behind them. The next panel shows the ship blowing up; parts of the ship are represented as black silhouettes against a white light. Moore and Gibbons have provided enough visual clues to link this sequence to the recurring image of the Hiroshima silhouette lovers.

Most of Chapter XI recounts the origins of Adrian Veidt. Interestingly, Veidt is almost always portrayed in his origin flashbacks as a silhouette. Is this an attempt to link him visually to Hiroshima, since he is about to perpetrate another mass murder? Once Veidt in the flashbacks assumes his super-heroic identity, he is no longer seen in silhouette but is shown only from the back, concealing his face.

Speaking of his hero Alexander the Great, Veidt says, "I wanted to match his accomplishment, bringing an age of illumination to a benighted world." But so far light – illumination – has been associated in *Watchmen* with destruction.

The scene shifts to New York, where lovers Joey and Aline quarrel. They appear in one panel with the spray painted silhouettes of embracing lovers. Perhaps this is to contrast the closeness of the silhouetted couple with the estrangement between the living pair, or perhaps it is an omen foreshadowing their impending death.

At the bottom of page nine, the protagonist in *The Black Freighter* comes ashore, where he will wreak the death of innocents. The first panel of the next page segues to Veidt in silhouette, walking out of the Black Sea in flashback. The *Black Freighter* narrator is paralleled with Veidt, who similarly has become so obsessed with his goal that he will kill innocents to achieve it. We cannot see Veidt's facial features in this panel, making it easier to identify him with the *Black Freighter* narrator, as if they have become one character.

On page 18, Veidt asks Nite Owl and Rorschach, "Ever read J.F.K.'s intended speech [that he was to give in Dallas the day of his assassination]? 'We in this country, in this generation, are by destiny, rather than choice, the watchmen on the walls of world freedom.'" Here Moore seems clearly to link the costumed heroes, and Veidt in particular, with America and its postwar mission to serve as the world's policeman, the guardians of freedom.

Veidt reveals to Rorschach and Nite Owl his master plan: to teleport his genetically-engineered squidlike creature into Manhattan where, dying, it will emit a "psychic shockwave" to kill half the city's population. Convinced this is the first attack in an alien invasion, the United States and Soviet Union will put aside their enmity and join forces to resist this seeming extraterrestrial threat.

Although the massacre is not caused by a nuclear explosion, Moore and Gibbons visually depict the shockwave as if it were just that. In the top tier of page 28 are panels showing familiar characters, mostly in pairs, looking towards a growing light that becomes white. Bernard the news dealer and Bernie the comics fan become silhouettes and embrace as the white light surrounds them. They have become another Hiroshima-style couple, and the light seems to dissolve their merged silhouettes, as if disintegrating them. The third panel is all white, suffused with this light. The panel can be also interpreted as a void. Moore and Gibbons represent the massacre as if it were another Hiroshima.

This light that brings death is the "illumination" that Veidt has actually brought to the world. In an interview, Veidt declares "I see the twentieth century as a race between enlightenment and extinction." In seeking to save the world and bring about "enlightenment," Veidt has unleashed a light that has caused the extinction of millions.

The cover and opening six pages of the final chapter survey ground zero of the Manhattan massacre. In his interview, Veidt referred to the Four Horsemen of the Apocalypse, and in these pages we see the dead attendees of the Pale Horse concert at Madison Square Garden. Streams of blood run down a clock showing midnight. This image visually echoes the Comedian's bloodstained button but also echoes the shattered watch on the cover of *Time*'s Hiroshima Week issue. A sign for the Promethean Cab company announces its motto, "Bringing Light to the World." Prometheus is the Titan in Greek mythology who gave humanity the gift of fire. Veidt perceives himself as humanity's benefactor but has just slaughtered millions with a "light" resembling the fires of a nuclear blast.

Later, Veidt lures Dr. Manhattan, along with Veidt's genetically-engineered feline Bubastis, into another intrinsic field subtractor. When Veidt activates the subtractor, both Dr. Manhattan and Bubastis become silhouetted, disintegrated skeletons engulfed by white light, visually echoing both Dr. Manhattan's origin and the Hiroshima silhouettes. The pair make the strangest shadow couple yet, united in death. (Veidt looks more distraught over sacrificing Bubastis than he ever does over human deaths.)

Boasting that the others have failed to stop his master scheme, Veidt again uses the symbolism of light: "You usher in an age of illumination so dazzling that humanity will reject the darkness in its heart."

The Faustian Conundrum

Confronted by a resurrected Dr. Manhattan, Veidt shows, on his wall of video screens, that the United States and Soviet Union have indeed ended hostilities to join forces against this perceived alien threat. Previously, Dan and Laurie spoke about the children killed at Hiroshima. One of the newscasters on Veidt's video screen now speaks of "the dead, the insane. There are children...

children, children... I can't go on. I'm sorry. I'm so sorry." Veidt, however, is not sorry. He exults, "I did it!"

Veidt points out that if the others expose the truth behind this supposed alien invasion, they will set the world back on the path to nuclear war. Dr. Manhattan, Nite Owl, and Silk Spectre all agree to keep silent, although the latter two are morally repulsed by the massacre. Perhaps Moore here means to parallel the general American acceptance of the bombing of Hiroshima and Nagasaki. The rationale for that horror is that the alternative would have been far more horrific. In an August 2003 column in *The New York Times*, Nicholas D. Kristof argued:

> Without the atomic bombings, Japan would have continued fighting by inertia. This would have meant more firebombing of Japanese cities and a ground invasion, planned for November 1945, of the main Japanese islands. The fighting over the small, sparsely populated islands of Okinawa had killed 14,000 Americans and 200,000 Japanese, and in the main islands the toll would have run into the millions.

Despite the continuing, adamant opposition of the Japanese military, "In the aftermath of the atomic bombing, the emperor and peace faction finally insisted on surrender and were able to prevail." Kristof quotes Hisatsune Sakomizu, Japan's chief cabinet secretary in 1945, as saying "The atomic bomb was a golden opportunity given by heaven for Japan to end the war." Attributing the devastation of two cities to God goes further even than Veidt in using religious imagery to justify his atrocities: "I saved Earth from hell. Next, I'll help her towards utopia." Kristof concludes,

> It feels unseemly to defend the vaporizing of two cities, events that are regarded in some quarters as among the most monstrous acts of the 20th century. But we owe it to history to appreciate that the greatest tragedy of Hiroshima was not that so many people were incinerated in an instant, but that in a complex and brutal world, the alternatives were worse.

But Nite Owl is aware that in condoning Veidt's scheme, he has made a Faustian bargain: "We're damned if we stay quiet, Earth's damned if we don't."

The distraught Laurie reacts to the horror of mass death in Manhattan by gaining a new awareness of the value of life: "Oh, it's sweet. Being alive is so damn sweet." She tells Dan, "I want you to love me because we're not dead." They embrace, and the last panel on page 22 shows their immense shadows embracing behind their small figures in long shot. The shadows evoke the Hiroshima silhouettes, but this time there is no danger or death. In Dan's dream, he and Laurie were dwarfed by the mushroom cloud of an atomic blast that annihilated them, but here it is their embracing shadows, a symbol of their love, that dominate the background. Rather than showing the brilliant light of an atomic blast, the panel is dimly lit, and the foreground dominated not by fire but by water, signifying life rather than destruction. The Hiroshima-style silhouettes were images of love after the lovers were killed. The silhouettes in this panel are cast by lovers who have survived, whose love and life go on in a sign of hope.

This panel, with Dan and Laurie's shadows, segues to a shot of Rorschach: the blots on his mask somewhat resemble the joined silhouettes of Dan and Laurie. But Moore and Gibbons seem here to contrast Dan and Laurie's reaction to Veidt's plot with that of Rorschach.

As a boy, Walter Kovacs approved of the U.S. rationale for the atomic bombing of Japan. But Rorschach refuses to keep silent when Veidt uses the same rationale to justify the Manhattan massacre. Why has Rorschach changed his mind?

Surely, in part, it is because Kovacs' sense of morality has radically changed since his boyhood. Rorschach has already claimed that in the early days of his costumed career he was "Very naive...very young," and not truly Rorschach yet: "Being Rorschach takes certain kind of insight." Rorschach supposedly believes in moral absolutes: he sees only black and white, not the grays in between. But Rorschach paradoxically justifies his own violations of the law – operating as a vigilante in defiance of the Keene Act, torturing informants, and murdering criminals – as serving a higher justice. For him, the end justifies the means. So how is Rorschach that different from Veidt, or from Truman and the others responsible for the bombing of Hiroshima?

The sheer scale of the massacre planned by Veidt overwhelmed the Comedian's cynically absurdist worldview. Unable to laugh off the murder of millions, Blake was left a broken man. Similarly, the scale of the Manhattan massacre proves too much for Rorschach to excuse. Though Veidt claims to have saved billions of people, the deaths of millions are too great a price to pay in Rorschach's view. He declares that he refuses to compromise his morality, "not even in the face of Armageddon." Once again, Moore invokes the end of the world, pointedly using a Biblical term. Does Rorschach think there must have been another way to prevent nuclear war? Or is Rorschach suggesting it's better to let humanity perish than to commit mass murder in an effort to prevent human extinction? Paradoxically, although Rorschach's insistence on exposing Veidt's guilt can seem heroic, if he sets the world back on the path to nuclear war as a result, Rorschach is arguably a greater threat to humanity than Veidt was.

Unwilling to compromise, Rorschach becomes the immovable object, opposed by the unstoppable force of Dr. Manhattan. Rorschach prefers being annihilated to surrendering the moral stand he has taken.

Arguably, the image of Rorschach's body as it disintegrates is another visual reference to the Hiroshima shadows. Colorist John Higgins colored it blue, not black, differentiating it from the previous shadows. But Higgins also indicated a burst of light, especially through the white area over most of Rorschach's body. Here is yet another deadly form of "illumination."

As Dr. Manhattan reenters Veidt's fortress, we are given snatches of news broadcasts from Veidt's video wall, including "Have described the scene as 'Hiroshima but with buildings,'" making the comparison between the two events explicit.

Dr. Manhattan finds the nude figures of Dan and Laurie, asleep after making love by the side of the pool: they are not shadows nor silhouettes, and are lit by the reflected green color of the water, not by blazing lights. Dr. Manhattan smiles in approval. The bombing of Hiroshima killed lovers, turning them into shadows; this living nuclear weapon spares these lovers.

Before the book takes leave of him, Veidt describes himself as if he had willingly become the scapegoat to bear the burden of guilt for what he contends was the necessary evil to avert nuclear war: "Someone had to take the weight of that awful, necessary crime." In the book's final picture of Veidt, he stands before his own black shadow, his head turned aside as if he cannot look at it. In order to save the world, Veidt has damned himself, and has thus become another victim of his new Hiroshima, another of the shadows.

Whether by intention or not, Veidt's massacre echoes the end of the 1962 novel *Fail-Safe* by Eugene Burdick and Harvey Wheeler, adapted into a 1964 film directed by Sidney Lumet. An American bomber mistakenly annihilates Moscow with nuclear bombs; to placate the Soviet Union and avert nuclear war, the President of the United States feels forced to detonate a nuclear bomb in New York City. The film concludes with a montage of ordinary New York citizens, each coming to an abrupt halt, signifying the explosion of the bomb. This parallels the gathering of familiar minor characters at the end of the penultimate chapter of *Watchmen*.

Another echo, coincidental or not, can be found in Peter Hyams's 1984 film *2010*, an adaptation of Arthur C. Clarke's novel *2010: Odyssey Two*, sequel to the novel and film *2001: A Space Odyssey*. The space mission in the film *2010* takes place against the background of the United States and the Soviet Union moving to the brink of nuclear war. (Although a visionary, Clarke did not foresee the collapse of the Soviet Union.) When alien monoliths transform the planet Jupiter into a second sun, the superpowers cease hostilities and join together. In both the film and book of *2010*, the alien intervention is no fraud. Indeed, according to the last line from the film, "We have been given a new lease – and a warning – from the landlord."

Towards the end of *Watchmen*, we see elements of a happy ending: Dan and Laurie are a happy couple under new identities, and Laurie reconciles with her mother. It is Christmas, and a card reading "Peace on Earth" is on display. In New York City, workmen remove spray-painted Hiroshima-style silhouettes of dead lovers from walls. It is as if the spectre of the deaths at Hiroshima and Manhattan are already fading in a world newly at peace.

But then comes the last silhouette: Seymour, as he enters the offices of the right-wing *New Frontiersman*. Seymour's arrival looks appropriately ominous because he may change the course of fate in the book's final panel, if he chooses Rorschach's journal to publish. In yet another possible coincidence, this is reminiscent of the final shot of the classic 1949 British black comedy *Kind Hearts and Coronets*, in which a serial murderer realizes he has inadvertently left behind a written confession in the form of a personal memoir; if someone finds and reads it, his crimes will be revealed.

A Film without Shadows

In director Zack Snyder's 2009 movie of *Watchmen*, Veidt kills not only much of the population of New York City, but also millions in other cities, including Los Angeles, London, Paris, Moscow, and Beijing. The film's Veidt does not employ a monster, such as the Lovecraftian squidlike creature in the book, to fake an alien attack. Instead, Veidt succeeds in duplicating Dr. Manhattan's unique form of energy and uses it to wreak physical devastation on sections of major cities. (Attentive viewers will note that the name of Veidt's energy research project bears the acronym SQUID.)

This change could have been meant to increase the similarity between the Manhattan massacre and the bombing of Hiroshima. Dr. Manhattan is figuratively a living nuclear bomb; by duplicating his energy, Veidt destroys sections of major cities with nuclear energy. (There does not seem to be lethal radiation remaining after the blasts, however: the film's New York City is not evacuated.) However, the *Watchmen* movie ignores the Hiroshima references and parallels. Hiroshima and Nagasaki are never mentioned; the spray-painted shadows of lovers never appear. Images in the original comics resembling the Hiroshima shadows, like Jon's disintegrating body or Nite Owl and Silk Spectre in Dan's nightmare, look very different in the film.

Rather, the filmmakers seem instead to draw a parallel between Veidt's massacres and the 9/11 attack on New York City's World Trade Center. The immense hole shown towards the end of the film may be where Times Square once was, but it is unmistakably reminiscent of "Ground Zero," the site of the World Trade Center in lower Manhattan.

(Curiously, one relevant historical reference not present in the comic is added for the film. The montage in the opening credits pays homage to a famous photograph by Alfred Eisenstaedt of V-J Day in Times Square, depicting an American sailor kissing a nurse amid the crowd celebrating the Allied victory in Japan; in the film version, the male sailor is replaced by the lesbian hero, the Silhouette.)

The Concluding Choice

The ending of *Watchmen* has repeatedly been criticized. Some readers find the squidlike monster too fantastical. Some readers object to Moore's use of a feigned extraterrestrial attack as a plot device. Perhaps such objections help explain why Snyder altered the ending for the film. Arguably, Veidt faking an attack by Dr. Manhattan is an improvement.

But Veidt's attack, whichever form it takes, is essential to the story. As noted at the beginning of this essay, *Watchmen* is a graphic novel about America, using the rise and evolution of the super-hero comment upon the development of the United States into a superpower from the 1940s to the 1980s. As Nite Owl asks, "What's happened to America? What's happened to the American dream?" – to which the Comedian replies, "It came true. You're lookin' at it."

Watchmen poses the question of whether one of the world's dominant superpower nations may sometimes have to commit an "awful, necessary crime" for the purpose of the greater good. The bombing of Hiroshima is an important motif because it is such an awful crime, yet one which may indeed have been necessary. It can be regarded as the American empire's original sin, by which the United States won World War II and firmly established its new position as one of the world's dominant powers and as a policeman of the world.

Moore compares Veidt's massacre to a second Hiroshima. In one sense, the massacre is a horrific means of balancing the scales, as in *Fail-Safe*: America pays for the destruction of Hiroshima and Nagasaki by losing half the population of its greatest city. Through Veidt's actions, Moore shows the rationale for the bombing of Hiroshima applied against America itself: President Truman bombed Hiroshima to bring the war to a quick end, preventing even greater bloodshed, and Veidt is willing to slaughter millions in order to save the lives of billions and human civilization itself.

Rather like Dr. Manhattan, Moore and Gibbons do not seem to either condone or condemn Veidt's decision. Instead, they present a variety of reactions through their main characters. Veidt fervently supports his actions, although he also feels pangs of guilt and horror. Dr. Manhattan coolly and logically evaluates Veidt's scheme, neither condemning nor condoning it – but refusing to expose it. Rorschach vehemently opposes Veidt. Nite Owl and Silk Spectre feel moral revulsion towards the massacre but are persuaded not to undo the world's chance for peace by exposing his guilt. Ultimately, it is up to the readers to decide which character they agree with.

Moore seems to use Veidt's faux alien attack to demonstrate that the "watchmen" of our world, whether self-appointed individuals like Veidt and the other heroes or officials of "superpower" governments, will continue to face the moral question that underlay the decision to bomb Hiroshima: whether the end ever justifies the means. In *Watchmen*, Richard Nixon and his administration face their own version of this dilemma: should they launch a preemptive nuclear strike on the Soviet Union, at the cost of the annihilation of the East Coast in response? "Would our losses be acceptable?" asks Nixon. (In the comic, Nixon is troubled by the prospect of millions of American deaths, though in the film he is actually pleased by the thought of the East Coast's destruction.) The situation is reminiscent of the Cuban Missile Crisis of 1962, although Nixon, unlike John F. Kennedy, makes no attempt to negotiate peace until after the Manhattan massacre. Similarly (as noted earlier), Moore links America's controversial Vietnam War to Hiroshima.

Although *Watchmen*, primarily set in 1985, may now seem like a period piece, the issue of whether immoral means can be justified to achieve a higher good remains relevant. The moral dilemma behind the Hiroshima bombing will continue to resurface in other circumstances. For example, in discussing America's use of torture in the current "War on Terror," James Fallows, a columnist for *The Atlantic*, wrote in February 2010: "Through American history, there have been episodes of brutality and abuse that, in hindsight, span a very wide range of moral acceptability." Fallows continues,

> But – to use the extreme case – America's use of the atomic bomb in Hiroshima and Nagasaki will always be the subject of first-order moral debate, about whether any "larger good" (forcing an end to the war) could justify the immediate suffering, the decades-long aftereffects, and the crossing of the "first use" frontier that this decision represented.

Fallows asserts that "anyone who is serious in endorsing the A-bomb decision has to have fully faced the consequences." He states this is why John Hersey's *Hiroshima*, a nonfiction book reporting on the bombing of the city and its aftermath, "was requisite basic knowledge for anyone arguing for or against the use of the bomb." Fallows then refers to the United States Justice Department's Office of Professional Responsibility's report on Bush administration lawyers Jay Bybee and John Yoo writing memos justifying the government's use of torture. "The OPR report is essentially *this era's* 'Hiroshima.' [Fallows's italics] As Hersey's book does, it makes us confront what was done in our name – 'our' meaning the citizens of the United States."

Watchmen likewise makes its readers confront what has been done in America's name for such noble purposes as battling aggressors and ensuring world peace. Veidt's massacre is a science-fictional counterpart of the bombing of Hiroshima, the war in Vietnam, and a potential preemptive attack on the Soviet Union – a real possibility in 1962: all examples of the wreaking of death on a massive scale to achieve peace.

But *Watchmen* also asks its readers to consider the individual's responsibility for moral decisions. There is Veidt's masterminding of the Manhattan massacre, and its parallel, in *Tales of the Black Freighter*, the mariner's increasingly self-deluded and bloodthirsty attempt to save his family and town. Wearing stars and stripes on his costume, as if a sinister version of Captain America, the Comedian killed alleged enemies on behalf of the government. Rorschach used torture and murder against those he perceived as criminals. Even Dan Dreiberg and Laurie Jupiter defy the law in resuming their costumed identities as Nite Owl and Silk Spectre. One can use immoral means for arguably moral ends by keeping silent about a crime, as Dan and Laurie do about Veidt's role in the Manhattan massacre.

Who watches the Watchmen? *Watchmen* asks its readers to watch them, whether they are the costumed super-heroes of the series, the lone mariner who sees himself as defender of his town against pirates, or the President of the United States. By extension *Watchmen* asks the reader to watch himself, to carefully weigh the consequences of his actions, lest in figuratively serving the cause of heaven, one ends by damning himself. In a series that often invokes religious imagery, the bombing of Hiroshima, burning its victims, could also be seen as a foreshadowing of Armageddon and, as the fallout shelter sign suggested, hell on Earth.

Works Cited

Chomsky, Noam, "The Responsibility of Intellectuals," *New York Review of Books*, February 1967

Fallows, James, "The OPR report: this era's 'Hiroshima,'" *The Atlantic* web site, February 21, 2010: theatlantic.com/politics/archive/2010/02/the-opr-report-this-eras-hiroshima/36313/

Kristof, Nicholas D., "Blood on Our Hands?," *The New York Times*, August 5, 2003: nytimes.com/2003/08/05/opinion/05KRIS.html

Paley, William, *Natural Theology, or Evidences of the Existence and Attributes of the Deity collected from the Appearances of Nature* (1802)

United States Department of Energy: Office of History & Heritage Resources, "The Manhattan Project: An Interactive History": "Potsdam and the Final Decision to Bomb, July 1945" cfo.doe.gov/Me70/manhattan/potsdam_decision.htm

United States Department of Energy: Office of History & Heritage Resources, "The Manhattan Project: An Interactive History": "The Atomic Bombing of Hiroshima, August 6, 1945" cfo.doe.gov/Me70/manhattan/hiroshima.htm

Somebody Has to Save the World: Captain Metropolis and Role-Playing *Watchmen*

by Timothy Callahan

Once, *Watchmen* wasn't considered a holy text worthy of hermetic study. It wasn't an unassailable masterpiece – a graphic novel of such importance that the mere mention of tie-in or spin-off products sends readers into an uproar. In 1987, it was just another DC comic – a special one, definitely, and one that seemed the harbinger of a new kind of super-hero story – but not one so special that it was above the same treatment as the costumed melodrama of *The New Teen Titans*, the space operatic hijinx of *The Legion of Super-Heroes*, or the post-apocalyptic Western strangeness of *Hex*. Like all three of those comics, *Watchmen* was fodder for role-playing games.

The *Watchmen* role-playing modules and sourcebooks published by Mayfair Games expanded the world created by Alan Moore and Dave Gibbons, and to this day they are the only narrative *Watchmen* spin-off products. Endorsed at the time by both Moore and Gibbons, the three Mayfair *Watchmen* volumes – *Who Watches the Watchmen*, *Taking Out the Trash*, and the *Watchmen Sourcebook* – present material only hinted at in the original 12-issue

DC series, and they provide information that elucidates many aspects of the story, the characters, and their world.

But before we explore how these authorized *Watchmen* supplements came to be, it's time to talk about a character who appears prominently in the Mayfair modules but was practically eliminated from the Zack Snyder *Watchmen* movie. It's time to talk about a character central to Moore and Gibbons's story, the man who inadvertently set Adrian Veidt's apocalyptic plan in motion, yet someone so rarely mentioned in relation to the series that thousands of new readers who rushed out to buy the *Watchmen* trade paperback in anticipation of the movie probably wouldn't even be able to identify him by name.

It's time to talk about Captain Metropolis.

The Essential Metropolis

In Snyder's movie, Captain Metropolis appears only in one scene, as an unidentified member of the Minutemen during the team's photo session. He is completely absent from what was originally his most important scene: Snyder transforms his role in gathering another group of costumed heroes he hopes to unite as "the Crimebusters" into Nite-Owl's leadership of the first meeting of a team called "the Watchmen." Thus, for those who know Moore and Gibbons's story through the film, Captain Metropolis faces the most ignoble of fates: obscurity.

The truth is, by reducing Captain Metropolis to a mere cameo appearance, Snyder strips *Watchmen* of the glue that holds it together.

Captain Metropolis is easy to overlook. Even if you've just finished reading the book, you might not recall exactly how often he appears. But Nelson Gardner, a.k.a. Captain Metropolis, pops up in almost every chapter – eight out of 12, to be precise. His presence lingers not because he is enigmatic like Ozymandias or omnipotent like Dr. Manhattan or scary crazy like Rorschach... but because he is so relentlessly eager. Like the Comedian, he forms an explicit link between the Minutemen of the past and whatever remains of the heroes of the present. But he's the flip side of the Comedian – soft and earnest where Edward Blake is hard and cynical.

The first time he appears in *Watchmen*, Captain Metropolis is just another member of the Minutemen. He doesn't even have any dialogue in the first flashback from Chapter II, and he's relatively nondescript. He looks like a generically handsome, square-jawed super-hero, kind of a young William Holden in crime-fighting drag. His blonde hair makes him stand out somewhat; the only other male super-hero of that era with exposed hair (though much darker) is the Comedian – a visual cue that links the pair together but shows an immediate visual contrast between them.

The second flashback in Chapter II is the more important one, at least where Captain Metropolis is concerned, because we get to see him in action. Sort of. In what we later find out is a flashback to 1964, he has gathered together the main characters for the "first ever meeting of the Crimebusters." Thicker at the waist, this older Captain Metropolis doesn't get very far into the meeting before being undermined by the Comedian, who mocks him by calling him "Nelly" and accusing him of "playin' cowboys and Indians." The scene ends with his grand plans literally going up in flames when the Comedian sets fire to his Crimebusters chart featuring labels for all of the social ills of the time, such as "promiscuity," "drugs," and "black unrest." As the meeting falls apart and the "heroes" leave, poor Nelson Gardner frantically calls out, "Somebody has to do it, don't you see? Somebody has to save the world..."

Nelson Gardner's inept leadership of the never-quite-Crimebusters offers more than just a chance to show the main characters in their younger days. That failed Crimebusters meeting is the lynchpin for the *Watchmen* story. It quickly establishes the different philosophies of each character: the Comedian is cocky and belligerent, Nite Owl is sincere, Rorschach (still sane) is skeptical of large groups, Ozymandias is idealistic, Silk Spectre is passive and unsure, and Dr. Manhattan is a dispassionate observer. All of these aspects of their personalities will be enhanced as the story moves on, but the Crimebusters scene shows them in relation to one another and shows the characters interacting as a group for the one and only time.

The same moment is also pivotal in establishing how Moore and Gibbons intend to dissect some of the unexamined assumptions of super-hero comics. Before *Watchmen*, the notion that super-heroes, given the opportunity, would unite in groups to fight evil more effectively was taken as a given, almost sacrosanct. Whole stories were built around new applicants eagerly seeking a place on the roster of the Justice League of America or the Justice Society or the Legion of Super-Heroes or the Avengers. *Watchmen* instead suggested that, looked at differently, the whole thing might seem ridiculous and heroes would have no part of it. Captain Metropolis thus becomes the voice representing how things had always worked in super-hero comics, genuinely puzzled and hurt that a newer generation might see it another way.

That one starring scene for Captain Metropolis appears again and again in *Watchmen,* as the failed Crimebusters meeting is revisited and retold from multiple points of view. For Rorschach, it was the meeting at which he admired and began to adopt the Comedian's uncompromising attitude. For Silk Spectre and Dr. Manhattan, it was where they first met and fell in love (such as it was). For Ozymandias, it was the spark that would lead to the entire conspiracy unfolded within the book. "Somebody has to save the world," said Captain Metropolis, and Ozymandias – the other blond costumed character in the book – took on the challenge, in his own morally suspect way. The failure of the Crimebusters meeting frames the dilemma facing Ozymandias: if a small group of costumed heroes couldn't unite toward a common goal, how can entire nations unite for the cause of world peace?

Captain Metropolis appears at other times in *Watchmen*: mentioned in Hollis Mason's memoir, popping up in framed photos on dressers, showing up at the Minutemen "reunion" at Sally Jupiter's house, out of costume, eager yet awkward, embarrassed by Sally's ribald stories – a relic from an out-dated era.

His costume – consisting of buttoned tunic, Art Deco insignia, cape, and Jodhpurs – call to mind an aviator hero from the pulps of the 1920s and 1930s, rather than the sleek tights-wearing of the comics, further positioning Captain Metropolis as a "retro" character with his roots firmly in the past. Designed to look old-fashioned to readers in 1986, it's possible to imagine he might already have looked a bit stuffy and out-of-fashion to his fellow Minutemen at their first meeting.

Captain Metropolis also serves as a link between comic-book fantasy and comic-book reality. Superman exists in the *Watchmen* universe but only in four-color form. As we learn from the memoirs of Hollis Mason, Superman's comic-book adventures inspired the first generation of "real-life" costumed heroes, and while Captain Metropolis might have taken his name from a Fritz Lang film, it's more likely that his name is an allusion to the fictional home of Superman, first named by Jerry Siegel and Joe Shuster in *Action Comics* #16 from September 1939.

Yet he's *Captain* Metropolis, the sickly child who would join the marines and apply military tactics to the war on crime. His name may partly allude to

Superman, but his name and origin also allude to Joe Simon and Jack Kirby's Captain America.

Captain Metropolis was also involved in a long-running relationship with the first costumed hero of the *Watchmen* world, Hooded Justice. Although Sally Jupiter indirectly refers to two gay members of the Minutemen in her interview which appears as a text supplement to the end of Chapter Eight, and another text piece talks about "Nelly" and "H.J." acting like "an old married couple," none of that information – his origin or his sexual orientation – is directly stated within the comic itself.

Instead, it was discussed in the Alan Moore-sanctioned role-playing game supplements, produced by Mayfair Games as part of their "DC Heroes" line.

Tabletop Crimefighting

In 1987, you could crack open a few role-playing game modules and act out the exploits of such DC Comics heroes as Wonder Woman, Firestorm, Metamorpho, the Comedian, or Ozymandias. You could kick ass playing Batman, or you could be Rorschach instead.

Watchmen was not on a towering pedestal back in those days, and it had merchandise. For $25 dollars, fans could purchase a water-resistant quartz watch with lime green hands and the familiar blood-spattered smiley badge as its face. If that was too pricey, a mere five dollars bought four metal pin-on badges mounted on a cardstock backing. One badge depicted a rorschach blot, another was the clock with dripping blood motif from the back covers of the comics, one was the black-and-yellow symbol warning of nuclear radiation, and the last bore the Latin motto "Ego Ipse Custodes Custudio," offering an appropriate variation on the quote from Juvenal. (The actual blood-splashed Comedian badge was not included with this collection.)

But if you wanted merchandise that offered more lasting entertainment value, there were the role-playing game supplements from Mayfair Games.

In the first role-playing game, *Who Watches the Watchmen* by Dan Greenberg, Captain Metropolis was the star. Greenberg began work on the adventure long before *Watchmen* reached its serialized completion – indeed, before the general public had heard of it. "I started work on the game when *Watchmen* was a three-page outline," Greenberg explained in a 2008 interview, "and published it a little more than halfway through the original 12-issue run of the comic book masterpiece."

For 4-6 Characters Generated Using 250-500 Hero Points   227

HEROES ROLE PLAYING MODULE

WATCHMEN

by Dan Greenberg

Who Watches the Watchmen?

A troubled Captain Metropolis assembles what he hopes will be a more successful second meeting of the Crimebusters. Cover art by Dave Gibbons from the Mayfair Games role playing module *Who Watches the Watchmen* (1987). Copyright © DC Comics.

Ray Winninger, now a senior director at Microsoft, wrote the follow-up *Watchmen* role-playing module *Taking Out the Trash* and created the 128-page *Watchmen Sourcebook*. Winninger had a similar timeline to Greenberg for his first book, though he'd seen at least a few issues of the actual comic before he started writing his spin-off. "I started *Taking Out the Trash* very early in the series's lifecycle, around the time issue #3 was released," Winninger said. "By that point, Alan had written up through around issue #8 or #9, but he knew exactly how everything would end."

Looking back more than 20 years later, Winninger added that he had always hated the title *Taking Out the Trash*. His original title was *The Harlot's Curse*, which would have referenced the William Blake poem Winninger had layered into the text of his game, but that seemingly less-commercial title was, according to Winninger, "changed by an overzealous Mayfair editor."

Greenberg, who has written a wide variety of role-playing game supplements in his long career, initiated the *Watchmen* project at Mayfair, and he did so for a couple of reasons. "I was a major fan of Alan Moore in the early '80s, and I thought his approach to the super-hero could invigorate the super-hero RPG." By 1986, Mayfair's DC Heroes line had already published over a dozen more traditional super-hero adventure modules set in the mainstream continuity of DC Comics, featuring the likes of the Justice League of America, Firestorm, and the Legion of Super-Heroes. Greenberg felt a *Watchmen* module had potential to be something much more than just another RPG spin-off: "I admired the way [Alan Moore] could not only shatter super-hero stereotypes but reintegrate them," said Greenberg. "I thought the RPG world could use a dose of that, too."

Greenberg set *Who Watches the Watchmen* in 1966 to avoid any overlap with the comic series. However, the role-playing adventure has striking parallels to *Watchmen*... parallels of which Greenberg was well aware, thanks to his behind-the-scenes access to Moore and Gibbons's work.

Who Watches the Watchmen opens with Captain Metropolis, who "broods on his failure" to get the Crimebusters off the ground and comes up with a plan to unite the heroes nonetheless and punch evil in its sorry face. As the Player Introduction explains:

> Just this morning, a series of bizarre kidnappings occurred. They started with the disappearance of Hollis Mason, the original Nite Owl, from his New York home. Then Wally Weaver, an associate of Dr. Manhattan's, disappeared from a heavily-protected military base. Shortly after the

disappearance, Ben Charles, a police chief who cooperated with Ozymandias in a number of cases, vanished while walking to his police station.   Sally Jupiter, the original Silk Spectre, never showed up at a photography session and has been missing since.

In a particularly tragic case, twelve-year-old Jeffrey Iddings was abducted from his home just two days after Rorschach rescued him from a cruel kidnapping attempt.   Cindy Radway, an actress who has been seen with the Comedian, disappeared from her Fifth Avenue apartment.   Captain Metropolis' elderly mother, Matilda Gardner, was discovered missing from her Long Island home.

Police investigated, but no motive was established in any of the incidents[,] and no ransom notes were left. It is Friday, the day of the kidnappings. Captain Metropolis has called an emergency meeting of the heroes to discuss the problem.

As the game begins, none of the players are aware of what the Game Master secretly knows: that Captain Metropolis has hired underworld thugs to abduct these individuals, concealing his identity and planting clues to indicate the hand of crime-lord Moloch. Thinking Moloch is behind the kidnappings, the assembled heroes will bust up his crime ring and realize that united they can make the world a better place. This is clearly a small-scale version of the conspiracy Ozymandias pulls off in *Watchmen*, but with Captain Metropolis as the schemer.

The adventure ends with Captain Metropolis gathering the assembled heroes together once more, after rescuing their imperiled friends and loved ones – because in the role-playing universe, the good guys must always win. He says, "Since we did so well as a group, I'd like to propose that we continue working together – as the Crimebusters!" The game directions say, "Captain Metropolis turns to the group hopefully..."

Then it's up to the players. Do Nite Owl and Ozymandias and the Comedian join forces as a crime-busting super-team and go off into more adventures concocted by the Game Master? Do they enter a rift between universes and end up fighting alongside the Justice Society? Or do they turn on Captain Metropolis, spotting clues that expose him as the mastermind behind the kidnapping plots... a pathetic has-been who risked the lives of their family members just so he could keep playing "cowboys and Indians"?

Good old Captain Metropolis. How far he has fallen.

Even though *Who Watches the Watchmen* echoes the comic series thematically – and even though it's hard to imagine that anything involving *Watchmen* would ever seem like a risky business venture – Greenberg recalled,

"I set out to adapt *Watchmen* to the role-playing game format with the odds stacked against me." He added,

> I had to convince Mayfair Games to agree to publish the game [at a time] when *Watchmen* looked like a much bigger risk than game adaptations of DC's flagship characters. It was especially important to me that I land the project and to get it done right. I worked very hard to convince everyone – Mayfair and DC and Alan Moore and Dave Gibbons – to support my approach to *Watchmen* so we could publish simultaneously with the comic.

Superiors at Mayfair pointed out that Greenberg could probably create two RPGs with all the extra time and effort it would take to create a game based on a comic of unproven appeal that did not yet even exist. In response, demonstrating his conviction that the game would be a success, Greenberg offered Mayfair the further inducement that he would do all the work on the game without any advance payment.

But even after sacrificing time and money, Greenberg couldn't have written *Watching the Watchmen* alone. "I was only able to complete the RPG module on time with the extremely generous cooperation from Alan Moore and Dave Gibbons," said Greenberg.

> The tight schedule left little room for error in writing, designing, game testing, coordinating original art with Dave Gibbons, and securing approvals from Alan Moore, DC Comics, and Mayfair Games. As far as I know, this kind of day-and-date releasing had not been attempted in RPGs before. It took a lot of hard work and persistence, but in the end, it was more than worth it. RPG gamers would be able to play through the first and only Crimebusters mission months before they would be able to read the ending of the *Watchmen* comic. That way, players would have experienced Captain Metropolis committing a terrible act in the name of a greater cause before they read Ozymandias's terrible act for a greater cause. But where Captain Metropolis makes a mess of it in the RPG, Ozymandias learns from him and figures out how to make it work. This deepens the implication in the comic that Ozymandias begins to formulate his ideas about how to "save the world" after Captain Metropolis's abortive attempt to form a team of heroes. So the game not only grows out of the ending of the comic, but also foreshadows the ending of the comic.

Greenberg found Alan Moore extremely helpful, noting that he was particularly generous with his time and patience in providing detailed answers to Greenberg's inexhaustible questions. Greenberg recalled, "I was especially honored when he started calling me to talk about his latest ideas."

Ray Winninger had similar experiences with his collaborative efforts. "On all of our various DC Heroes projects we received a lot of cooperation from various DC creators, Alan and Dave included." Winninger continued,

> Shortly after I picked up the *Watchmen* assignment, I called Alan in Northampton. He was unbelievably nice and excited about the project. During that first call, he spent almost two hours telling me exactly what was about to happen in the next nine issues of the comic, down to the level of individual panels and page layouts.

Winninger still remembers Moore saying, "Right, Issue 12. We open with six pages of corpses." Winninger spoke with Moore several times thereafter to bounce his ideas for the role-playing adventure off Moore, to clarify details, and to get his approval on the manuscripts and such. Moore endorsed everything Winninger planned for the *Watchmen* role-playing game supplements. "I don't recall him ever vetoing anything. I certainly wouldn't have used anything he didn't like. He and I riffed together on some of the new stuff – backgrounds for some of the Minutemen is one detail I remember." And as Winninger points out, Dave Gibbons provided original cover art for the Mayfair *Watchmen* books and added new interior art as well.

Greenberg cites a few differences between working on a *Watchmen* book and the other DC Heroes game modules (which were based on characters who had existed in multiple incarnations over several decades), leading to a greater variety of possible approaches. "The restrictions were that I had to make sure all new material fit not only *Watchmen* continuity but also fit the world thematically. Depending on your interpretation, those rules constitute either a nearly impossible set of restrictions or near-total freedom. To me, they counted as near-total freedom."

Greenberg explained his story's evolution:

> The idea to have Captain Metropolis engineer a plot to force the characters to work together popped into my head in the middle of my first phone call to Alan Moore. I blurted out the idea while we were brainstorming, and he approved the plotline on the spot. He even made helpful suggestions which I adopted – like using Moloch as the logical fall guy for Captain Metropolis. Making Moloch a double patsy – first for Metropolis and then again for Ozymandias – could lend another layer of poignancy to the Moloch-Comedian scene in the comic. The map-burning scene was the perfect catalyst for a plot that delivered the things *Watchmen* players would want – the main characters in action together, political overtones with lots of potential for friction between the heroes, and a dark, twisted ending that turned heroism upside down. It fit my

sense of the themes of *Watchmen* to have the surprise ending of the game echo the surprise ending of the comic.

Along the way, Mayfair requested that Greenberg consider other approaches, such as Minutemen adventures, solo action for each hero, and smaller teams. According to Greenberg, suggestions included "Nite Owl and Rorshach versus criminals" (the approach taken by the downloadable video game released in 2009 for the Xbox 360 and Playstation 3 platforms as a movie tie-in), "Dr. Manhattan and Silk Spectre on patrol" (he's a living god, she can do gymnastics!), and even "the Comedian and Dr. Manhattan versus the Vietnamese," a suggestion which made Greenberg cringe. "But the clear winner was the idea of adding to established continuity and foreshadowing Ozymandias's plot with false flag kidnappings. Happily, it worked."

Greenberg took all of his Mayfair work seriously, but this was a very special project. He had been a huge fan of Alan Moore since the early '80s, when he chased down imports of U.K. titles such as *Warrior* every month to read the latest installments of the Moore-scripted "Marvelman" and "V for Vendetta." Chasing down such comics from overseas was, he notes, a lot more difficult in the pre-Internet era.

The Politics of Success

Winninger took a more politically-inspired approach when conceiving of the story FOR *Taking Out the Trash*. Fascinated by the fact that Richard Nixon was still President well into the 1980s, Winninger decided to build a story around Nixon and his rise to power. For *Watchmen*, a more mundane adventure about stopping Moloch from robbing a museum, or something along those lines, just didn't seem appropriate. This led Winninger to develop a storyline involving the heroes in a quasi-political thriller set against the backdrop of the 1968 Presidential election.

The role-playing in *Taking Out the Trash* opens with Rorschach and Nite Owl on one of their nightly patrols of the city. After rescuing an old man from assault by a gang called the Brethren in the New York subway system, they join the other heroes for a meeting with the Secret Service. The heroes are asked to provide additional security for the Republican National Convention, particularly against possible disruptions planned by none other than the Brethren. As the adventure unfolds, it turns out that the street gang has close connections with organized crime... and possibly even with a future candidate for President of the

United States. And of course, a President with ties to organized crime might be extremely useful to Moloch...

Taking Out the Trash goes even further than *Who Watches the Watchmen* in suggesting the distinctive creative approach of *Watchmen* itself within the game materials. Winninger's text includes such items as a reproduced letter from Adrian Veidt sharply criticizing an *Ozymandias* role-playing game he has been asked to approve, and even a note from Dr. Manhattan addressed to the Game Master, discussing information they share which no other players possess:

> You are going to skip the rest of the text in this column, and skip through the pages that follow. Eventually, you return to this introduction, out of curiosity about what I might say, and fear that you might have missed something...

This approach was taken to an extreme with the *Watchmen Sourcebook* in 1990. The *Sourcebook* plays out like an extended version of the text supplements that end each chapter of *Watchmen*, featuring notes and documents and other ephemera that expand on the stories of all the heroes. We learn a considerable amount of backstory for other previously overlooked characters, such as Mothman. (He turns out to have been a wealthy left-leaning civil rights crusader who got into a fistfight with Captain Metropolis in 1948, after the latter made derogatory racist comments during a visit to Harlem.) We also receive a few glimpses of more "recent" events, such as a newspaper clipping announcing the death of Edward Blake in a fall from his penthouse apartment during an attempted break-in, a tragic hint at his previously unseen final moments, and a driver's license issued to one Sandra Hollis. In some ways, the *Sourcebook* feels more like an appendix to *Watchmen* itself, and a great deal of the material it includes could be inserted into the comic as a postscript and not seem out of place.

Ray Winninger had similar feelings to Dan Greenberg about working on the *Watchmen* supplements:

> The *Watchmen* projects were very special to me right out of the gate. When I started writing them, nobody knew that *Watchmen* would become such a classic, but I loved the material I'd seen. I was already a huge fan of Alan Moore – I was following his *Swamp Thing* at the time – and I was looking forward to working with him and playing around with his concepts. Today I'm generally pretty happy with the sourcebook, but I'd love an opportunity to rewrite that adventure now that I'm older and wiser.

Winninger recalled that, in the beginning, Alan Moore didn't plan for *Watchmen* to be a self-contained book:

> Very early on, I remember that Alan was excited about extending *Watchmen* in various directions. I remember him mentioning a couple of things he was interested in – a *Tales From the Black Freighter* comic with Joe Orlando and some of the other old EC artists, and maybe a *Minutemen* miniseries. Obviously, his falling out with DC killed any possibility we'd ever see these projects, but I also got the sense he was starting to believe that perhaps *Watchmen* was better left alone.

Now, over 20 years later, the three Mayfair game supplements are the only existing expansions to the *Watchmen* universe. Their place in *Watchmen* history has raised their value over the decades, with the *Sourcebook* selling for over $100 in some online auctions. But even in the 1980s, the *Watchmen* books did very well for Mayfair Games. Greenberg was told by Mayfair that *Who Watches the Watchmen* was their hottest-selling module and broke sales records, leading them to quickly greenlight two more *Watchmen* titles. Greenberg notes that his contract disputes with Mayfair explain why Winninger, not Greenberg, worked on the last two books in the series. Greenberg adds that his module "got great reviews, terrific fan feedback, and won the RPG industry's top award." Winninger agrees with Greenberg's memory of the books' sales: "The *Watchmen* books were big sellers for us. They sold more than twice as much as an average DC Heroes product."

According to Greenberg, there were also interesting reactions from players who enacted the *Watchmen* adventures:

> In playtesting, I found that players sometimes made choices that echoed the actions their characters would take later in the comic, actions the players did not know about because those issues had not been published, and I didn't let any game testers see the notes about the ending of the comic. Just as Rorschach grew in the telling from a repellent creature to a figure of strange integrity, I found the same thing happening in playtests. His Ditkoesque "never compromise" approach was a constant source of inter-party friction and took the role-playing to a higher level.

Greenberg points out that the modules' success had an impact on Mayfair's later offerings:

> All the "mature" elements of the plot that Mayfair was so nervous about turned out to be among the strongest parts of the module. They were favorably reviewed, earned great player feedback, and were commended by retail stores and distributors who asked for more mature material. Not long after, Mayfair did a 180 and started work on its first line of 'edgy' games aimed at more mature audiences.

That line of "edgy" products included the game *Underground* which mixed together a band of genetically enhanced ex-mercenaries, politics, and cannibalism – a legacy the *Watchmen* creators probably never imagined (but that parallels *Watchmen*'s effect on super-hero comics).

Dan Greenberg is happy with the reception of his addition to the *Watchmen* milieu, but wanted to make one thing clear:

> I'm pleased that some fans like it so much they consider the events to be part of the *Watchmen* canon because it fits seamlessly and because Alan Moore approved it. But I have told them that I cannot agree with them. Only the *Watchmen* series itself is canon. My game is only an adaptation – reflected light and not the source.

Greenberg added, "I'm proud of *Who Watches the Watchmen*. I achieved just about everything I set out to achieve with it."

Ray Winninger also has nothing but affection for his work on the *Watchmen* RPG books: "Working on *Watchmen* was an absolute pleasure; the sourcebook in particular was probably the most interesting gaming project I had the opportunity to work on. I'm very pleased to be a little footnote in the *Watchmen* story."

Perhaps because he had more access to the complete *Watchmen* story, Winninger ends up as the author who was able to incorporate previously unknown Moore-sanctioned information in his two volumes. Here we learn of Nelson Gardner's Charles-Atlas-meets-Captain-America transformation from a sickly and unathletic youth, teased by other children, into a fit Marine and crime-fighter – a detail which makes his constant longing for a team of fellow adventurers to pal around with more telling and poignant. We also learn many background details of characters in "the World of Watchmen," an insert within the *Taking Out the Trash* module for which Alan Moore is credited as co-writer. That module not only explicitly identifies Captain Metropolis and Hooded Justice as a gay couple, but it also provides other information about these characters not directly mentioned in *Watchmen* itself. For instance, we learn that while his failure to appear before the House Un-American Activities Committee led to suspicions of Communism, Hooded Justice's membership in the Ku Klux Klan "is testimony to the fact that [Rolf] Muller was a staunch anti-communist." We also learn of tension between the Silhouette and Hooded Justice.

Perhaps most notably, the supplement solves the murder of Hooded Justice that *Watchmen* itself left ambiguous, stating that the Comedian secretly murdered Hooded Justice in 1955 out of revenge for the beating he received after raping Sally Jupiter. Such knowledge adds subtext to the Comedian's mockery and hostility toward Captain Metropolis in the 1964 Crimebusters meeting. And it comes straight from the mind of Alan Moore, even if none of this information appears in the pages of *Watchmen*.

Sometime between the release of Winninger's *Watchmen Sourcebook* in 1990 and today, *Watchmen* became deemed too pure to touch. Fans today would scoff at the idea of a *Watchmen* role-playing game – it would seem as silly as a *Citizen Kane* role-playing game… or a *King Lear* one. At this point, the characters are locked in their classic molds, and all you would be doing is playing out their inevitable fates.

Perhaps it's too early to say such things, though. When Deadline Games produced the *Watchmen: The End is Nigh* game as a movie tie-in, with a storyline written by *Watchmen* editor Len Wein and with Dave Gibbons as a creative consultant, the game incorporated additional characters and backstory taken directly from the Mayfair RPG games. Zack Snyder's movie version of *Watchmen* may not have made the half billion dollars the studio might have hoped for… but as long as Time Warner owns the rights to the story, isn't it possible that somewhere, sometime, someone will have the idea to take these characters out of mothballs and set them off on a new adventure? Is a massively multiplayer online role-playing game set in "The World of Watchmen" such a far-fetched idea?

And if it is not so far-fetched, how far would such a game go? Will everyone be expected to stick to the roles of Nite Owl, Silk Spectre, or Rorschach? Or if you choose, will you also get to be the gay, racist, prudish, old-fashioned, lonely Captain-America-meets-Charles-Atlas analogue whose fondest wish was simply to go on playing the role of hero?

Will you get to be Captain Metropolis?

The End is Nigh: The Limits of *Watchmen*

by Geoff Klock

In *The Culture of Narcissism: American Life in an Age of Diminished Expectations*, Christopher Lasch describes a family scenario:

> The narcissist... often occupies a special position in the family, either because of his real endowments or because one of the parents treats him as substitute for an absent father, mother, or spouse. Such a parent sometimes draws the whole family into the web of his neurosis, which the family members tacitly conspire to indulge so as to maintain the family's emotional equilibrium.

Is the family here the comic-book community? And is the child, which clearly has real endowments, *Watchmen*? The worship *Watchmen* receives from fans of super-hero comics is nearly universal. And yet it is entirely possible to be the best at something and still be overrated. There do exist complaints about *Watchmen* from super-hero fans, comic-book scholars, and from the larger non-comics world. Let us seriously consider four such complaints that are most often ignored, due to the book's absurdly high reputation: its damaging influence on comics, its pessimism, objections to the final plot twist, and the claim that the book, for all its reputation for maturity, is simply juvenile.

"*Watchmen* was great but it made me never want to read a super-hero comic again."

With the movie coming out, one of my friends who is not a comics reader wanted to check out *Watchmen*. He liked it but also said it made him never want to read another super-hero comic again. Many comic-book writers felt similarly impressed, overwhelmed, and defeated: the very existence of *Watchmen* made it very difficult to write good comics. *Watchmen* is a tremendously hard act to follow. Its narrative sophistication, noted by so many critics, raised the bar massively, making it one of the only super-hero comics to deserve the "novel" in "graphic novel." But that is a complex thing to digest — only incredible talent, nurtured by time, was going to be able to follow suit. What happened next was predictable: the easiest thing to copy was the violence, the gritty sense of the streets, the pessimism, the brooding narration, and the Nietzsche quotations. Alan Moore has remarked:

> The thing that I most regretted about *Watchmen*: that something that I saw as a very exciting celebratory thing seemed to become a kind of hair shirt that the super-hero had to wear forever after... [T]hey've all got to be miserable and doomed. That was never what me and Dave intended.

Influence is complex, and *Watchmen*'s influence is not limited to the works that come after it; because it persuades us to see differently, *Watchmen* also influences the way we look at the comics that came before, so potentially its influence is on the whole field, past, and present. Writing for Slate, Grady Hendrix remarks that *Watchmen* "became to comic books what *The Sopranos* is to TV: an intellectual fig leaf concealing the vast wasteland of *Two and a Half Men* reruns."

There are three objections tangled up here: that *Watchmen* misrepresents comics, that *Watchmen* deformed comics through its influence, and that *Watchmen* is a kind of aesthetic dead end. The first objection is absurd. There is no genre and no medium that does not have a quality ratio like this. Is *Ulysses* the intellectual fig leaf concealing the vast wasteland of *Da Vinci Code* reprints? Is *In the Aeroplane Over the Sea* the intellectual fig leaf concealing the vast wasteland of Fall Out Boy albums?

The second objection is equally pointless in its generality: great works of art deform the works that come later, as artists struggle to deal with the ramifications of this new, powerful force dominating the imagination. *Paradise Lost* blasted the poetic landscape for 150 years until Wordsworth managed to confront and revise it in his *Prelude*, and poets today wither in the shadow of

John Ashbery. You can hardly blame *Watchmen* for challenging future writers, especially since there will in any case only be a handful of geniuses – and like Wordsworth, they will be stronger for passing through Moore's gauntlet.

The third objection is more troubling: is *Watchmen* a kind of aesthetic dead end for the super-hero comic book? Carter Scholz reviewed *Watchmen* in *The Comics Journal* in 1988. The review came soon enough after the original publication of *Watchmen* not to be affected by the canonical place it would eventually hold in the comics community, and the *Journal* is importantly dedicated to a medium rather than a genre. Scholz said:

> I won't re-read it because it's too incestuous to repay that degree of attention. Moore has taken established comic book characters... and has done his manful best to make them real people, in a realistic milieu. This, of course, is what Stan Lee was renowned for (without much justification, if you ask me), and Moore is Lee-cubed, but without Lee's American hyperbole, optimism, and bounce. It makes for an altogether more refined performance, one which is more palatable to an adult mind, but it is essentially the same act, and I think it's a sterile one. In some ways[,] Moore's approach is the weaker, and the more radical – weaker, because the super-hero genre was never made to take the strain he puts on it, and the more radical because he has taken an untenable concept absolutely as far as it can go.

Certainly, it is hard to imagine comics being taken any farther in the direction that Moore took them. There is not much farther for the super-hero to fall before descending into the bathos of parody. The claim can always be made that it is too early to call, but consider James Joyce's *Finnegan's Wake*: an absurdly skillful work that does not seem to be a positive influence on anything because it is a total dead end, an apotheosis of language that fails to make the argument that it is necessary in any way to the future of the novel. If you look at the major post-super-hero works in the wake of *Watchmen*, they either nearly collapse under the weight of its influence (*Marvels, Kingdom Come*) or seem to get on by reacting against it totally, avoiding it, in such wonderfully optimistic and fertile works as *All-Star Superman* and *Casanova*.

In the end, *Watchmen*'s main power may simply be in the fact that it exists, even if closed off. We should remember the story about an artist who said he wanted to draw comics "the Kirby Way." According to Jack Kirby's former assistant Mark Evanier, upon hearing this Kirby responded that this guy had misunderstood – the Kirby way was to create something *new*, not set out to emulate anyone else. The true power of *Watchmen* rests in its perpetual promise that the super-hero comic can be used to make something powerful, personal, and revolutionary. Out of nowhere, the whole field can change – even from the effects *Watchmen* has wrought. Looked at in this way, *Watchmen* is an emblem of potential.

"*Watchmen*? What's that? Is that the one where the hero dog gets its head kicked in?"

One of the main complaints to be made about *Watchmen* is that it is depressing, pessimistic, cynical, and nihilistic. In its negative reviews on Amazon.com, this is the most common source of the single star ratings. Even a powerhouse like Grant Morrison can use this complaint to distance himself and his work from the crushing influence of Moore's major work. When Matt Brady from *Newsarama* asked if a sandwich-sign doomsayer, glimpsed in the opening of the concluding issue of Morrison's *Final Crisis* mini-series, was intended as a nod to Rorschach, Morrison sarcastically responded, "*Watchmen*? What's that? Is that the one where the hero dog gets its head kicked in? Sweet." It is a hard objection to deny.

Though it has moments of transcendent happiness – a couple falls in love, and there is a big happy face on the surface of Mars – one is still left with the overall feeling of something relentlessly grim: a story in which super-heroes are disturbed, evil, violent, escalate the arms race, act as their own villains, kill millions without punishment, sacrifice two of their own, and generally fail to care about the fates of regular people. We often describe how *Watchmen* does something serious and mature with this silly genre, in which people wear their underwear on the outside of their clothes, without feeling sympathy for people who want a little wonder and amazement and instead find themselves seeing some woman being raped and falling in love with her rapist.

But ultimately, the objection that *Watchmen* is depressing is as absurd as holding it responsible for its influence. It's like complaining ice cream has too much sugar. It refuses to confront the work on its own terms. *Watchmen* may be nihilistic, but the question is, among nihilistic fiction, does it stand up well? I think it pretty obviously does. Its nihilism is forceful and effecting – and pretty well thought-through.

Donald Barthelme once said that "no one who writes as well as Beckett can be said to be doing anything other than celebrating life." It takes only the

Cover art by Dave Gibbons from volume six of *Les Gardiens*. Each volume of this French edition, published in 1988 by Zenda, collected two translated issues of *Watchmen*. Copyright © DC Comics.

slightest change in our attitude toward the work to see it as uplifting on the formal, poetic, and imaginative – rather than narrative – level.

"Is this the best that the 'smartest man in the world' can come up with?"

Returning to Scholz's 1988 review in *The Comics Journal*, his next objection is significantly more persuasive than his first:

> It doesn't work because it's all too self-referring. Moore does real lapidary work here – there are many levels of carefully-designed subtleties throughout *Watchmen* – but most of them turn to point directly at the deficiencies of super-hero comics of the past, while maintaining as well as possible all the beloved old nonsense. We have the "world's smartest man" (what in the name of Gardner Fox does that mean?) who has a Fortress of Solitude at the South Pole, we have aging heroes wryly aware of the sexual element to their costumes, we have a bang-up treatment of the psychotic hero gone Ayn Rand – we have in short a brilliant doctoral dissertation on the super-hero comic. Only it isn't a dissertation; it's, perversely, a super-hero comic. And... we have the familiar Manichean plot, the crux of which is the fate of the world. And what a cruddy plot it turns out to be. The story finally devolves on Veidt's plan to save mankind from nuclear Armageddon by, here comes the crud, faking an alien invasion – a plot device that John W. Campbell would have laughed out of the *Astounding* slush pile 40 years ago. Is this the best that the "smartest man in the world" can come up with?

The first half of this is a more sophisticated form of the same objection we just examined, an objection not to the execution of the work but to the idea behind it. Like the Amazon.com reviewers taking *Watchmen* to task for being depressing, Scholz takes it to task for the way it includes elements of super-hero comics in order to "deconstruct" them as an academic dissertation on comics would. Most of this should be easily dismissed. The "aging heroes wryly aware of the sexual element to their costumes" is one of the most affecting, knowing, human, and persuasive parts of the book. In the second half, however, we confront a proper objection – in retaining elements of old super-hero comics, Moore's story is susceptible to the same complaints we would make about those elements in those earlier stories.

One way to confront Scholz here is to point out that the "Fortress of Solitude" and the "world's smartest man" claims are not quite the nonsense Scholz suggests they are. Both reflect how the character of Adrian Veidt has accumulated power and wealth by tapping into these ideas; he has, after all, built a career around marketing his previous super-hero persona, even down to a line of action figures. But there is another, larger sense here of what the problem is with Scholz.   More than 20 years later, in a 2009 blog post, Frank Santoro makes an extremely insightful claim about *Watchmen* that answers most of these objections:

> *Watchmen* is a Lutheran reformation text knocking on the door of the Catholic establishment... Why I think scholars of comics don't really enjoy it is because they aren't superhero fans. The text is an indictment of the form, the laws, by a believer in the form. I don't know if anyone who wasn't a "true believer" to start with really "gets" the full impact of the text. It's like a Muslim saying he doesn't enjoy the New Testament.

Scholz, not a believer in the genre, cannot understand the attention to all the elements of the super-hero comic book. He lacks a sensitivity that is necessary to understand *Watchmen* – except for the fake alien invasion. That is a real complaint. Like Veidt's Antarctic "Fortress of Solitude," his reputation as the "world's smartest man," and the costumes, this is absolutely an element of older comics Moore wanted to include as part of his radical take on comics history. He puts in something reflective of absurd science-fiction horror. But this is a crucial plot point, and one that strains credulity *within* the world Moore and Gibbons have built, in a way that the PR campaign of an egomaniac billionaire does not. The objection to the alien invasion *does* take the work on its own terms. Veidt's plan of teleporting an artificially-constructed, giant, telepathic, alien, vagina-rectum squid into Manhattan and killing millions in the process – thus ending the Cold War by giving the warring powers a common enemy to unite against – is basically successful, at least in the short term. This is how he wins. And as Scholz suggests, it is a pretty cruddy resolution.

It is important to note that this was the only major plot change in the *Watchmen* movie, which attempted – in spite of director Zack Snyder's worship of violence – to hew to the plot as closely as possible. Even sympathetic reviewers admitted that the squid would have been hard to take seriously on screen (without getting into the question of whether it can be taken seriously in the comic book). And for all the visual absurdity, we *are* supposed to take it seriously, because it caused the death of so many people. Splash page after splash page after splash page – used nowhere else in the book – show the carnage created by this thing. While some irony is obviously intended in the juxtaposition of the thing's design and the carnage, the primary reaction is to take seriously the death of so many people, so that we can evaluate the monstrous thing Veidt has done and grapple along with the other lead characters about how to judge him. We are clearly not supposed to allow the squid to sever our emotional engagement with the book. It is hard, though possible, to take seriously the death – all of *Watchmen*, after all, has prepared us for this moment by continually juxtaposing realistic violence and emotion with the trappings of old comics. But the world's reaction on Veidt's TV screens breaks the little world Moore has made, and not in some kind of intentional Brechtian way, I think. It is just dumb. It is only because Moore gets so much right in *Watchmen* that this flaw has been so consistently ignored. Perhaps Moore has earned the right to get this part wrong.

"The last time I looked, the only ones quoting Nietzsche were teenagers."

I read *Watchmen* for the first time when I was 19. Of course, it blew me away – as did Frank Miller's *The Dark Knight Returns*, which I read the next day. At 26, in graduate school, I read Tom Shone's review of *Watchmen* for the website Slate as part of the book's 20th anniversary, and I can still remember my palpable anger rising as I read it:

> Whether you take [*Watchmen*'s] self-reflexivity as evidence of a newfound sophistication on behalf of the comic book, or as self-hatred tricked out as superiority – that old adolescent standby – is up to you. *Watchmen* was unquestionably a landmark work, a masterpiece, even. Before Moore came along, comic books were not generally in the habit of quoting Nietzsche, or scrambling their time schemes, or berating their heroes for their crypto-fascist politics, or their readers for reading them. It was Moore's slightly self-negating triumph to have allowed it to do so. But did the comic book have to "grow up"? The last time I looked, the only ones reading *Ulysses* and quoting Nietzsche were teenagers. No adult has time for aesthetic "difficulty" or "self-consciousness." Life is too short. Frankly, we'd much rather be watching *The Incredibles*.

Had I been granted fantastic mental powers, Tom Shone's head would have simply exploded from a distance. I *did* take *Watchmen*'s self-reflexivity as evidence of a newfound sophistication on behalf of the comic book. Virtually all super-hero fans did – and do. But I did more than agree it was sophisticated. At the time I was reading Shone's review, I had pretty much devoted my life to difficult art – specifically aesthetically difficult poets such as Blake and Ashbery. "The last time I looked, the only ones reading *Ulysses* and quoting Nietzsche were teenagers" made me furious because he was implicitly saying that my adulthood and my profession – not to mention my own Nietzsche-quoting book – was nothing more than an extended adolescence and childish foolishness.

And yet.

I think the reason Shone made me so enraged was because deep down I knew that, while he overstated his case, what he was saying was true. I thought to defend myself by noting that the whole culture keeps people in an extended adolescence for a remarkably long time... but I still felt unsettled. Confronting Shone again now, at 30 – finished with graduate school and now a member of the work force – I feel a certain amount of sympathy with the sentiment. The last time I looked, the only ones reading *Ulysses* and quoting Nietzsche *were* teenagers. I still respect the hell out of David Lynch's difficult *Inland Empire*, but I have to admit I prefer *Grosse Point Blank*. And as much as I can see what a thing *Watchmen* is, it does seem angsty, over-serious, fussy, and pretentious.

Confronting what it means to be an adult was my goal in reading the Lasch book quoted at the opening of this essay. I wondered if it reflected how I was raised – a narcissist man-child with a house filled with comics and a mind filled with overblown expectations for what the adult world would hold for me. The gentle irony of the adult Shone preferring a kids movie – a kids movie influenced by *Watchmen,* no less, one that he might enjoy watching as an adult with his children – is not lost on me. It does seem more appealing than reading a book aimed at very smart, brooding teenagers.

Watchmen is stunning. I have a tremendous awe for what Moore did, and I would not argue against *Watchmen*'s place in the comic-book canon with a gun to my head. But I also feel that its self-seriousness belongs to an earlier part of my life. I respect it, but I no longer love it. Without it, I could never appreciate most of the comics I love now – probably none of them would have been written without *Watchmen* anyway. But *Watchmen* is a limited book, for a limited period in life – perhaps all books are. *Watchmen* appeals to kids (of whatever actual age) who think they are ready to grow up but don't know enough to know what that will be like. *Watchmen* is an exquisite creation appealing to adolescents by showing them the pinnacle of what they imagine an "adult" comic book would look like.

Like Shone, the books I want to read now are works that appeal to adults by showing them the pinnacle of what they imagine children's literature should look like: books such as Jack Kirby's Fourth World series and Grant Morrison and Frank Quitely's *All Star Superman*. It is no coincidence that both are hymns to youth and wonder always available to anyone, they promise – against the horrid stasis of old age. The Forever People versus Darkseid. Superman versus

Lex Luthor. Despite the fact that super-hero comics are marketed to college-educated adults, of course they are juvenile. That is part of what I *like* about them, and it seems like something I am going to need whether I remain in an extended adolescence or not.

Watchmen wants to transmute the camp and silliness of old comics into *a serious work of art for serious people...* and that just seems like something Darkseid would want to do.

Works Cited

Bartheleme, Donald. *Not-Knowing: The Essays and Interviews.* New York: Vintage, 1999

Brady, Matt. "Grant Morrison: *Final Crisis* Exit Interview Part 2." *Newsarama.* 4 February 2009. 12 April 2009

Evanier, Mark. "Afterword." *Jack Kirby's Fourth World.* Volume 1. New York: DC Comics, 2007

Heer, Jeet. "A *Watchmen* Dissent." *Sans Everything.* 4 March 2009. 12 April 2009

Hendrix, Grady. "*Watchmen* Failed." *Slate.* 9 March 2009. 12 April 2009

Lasch, Christopher. The Culture of Narcissism: American Life in an Age Diminishing Expectations. New York: Norton, 1979

Scholz, Carter. "Furriners." *The Comics Journal* #199. January 1988.

Shone, Tom. "Rereading *Watchmen.*" *Slate.* 5 March 2009 [reprinted from 2005]. 12 April 2009

Some Different Sort of Time: *Watchmen* as Cinema

by Patrick Meaney

Three months before its release in March of 2009, anticipation for the film version of *Watchmen* was running high both in the comic-book press and among the general public, who bought the book in huge numbers to prepare for the film's release. People talked about *Watchmen*, people read *Watchmen*, and excitement for Zack Snyder's cinematic adaptation couldn't have been higher. Three months after its release, however, discussion of the film was minimal. After 20 years of anticipation, the film vanished quickly from the cultural dialogue – neither loved nor hated by either the fanbase or general audiences.

The film itself has very little that is original to offer, but it does provide a new prism through which to view the original work. A film adaptation that's incredibly faithful in so many respects but ultimately hollow itself helps clarify what makes the original work so special, and it provides a template for subsequent filmmakers on how to best attain the artistic heights reached in a comic such as *Watchmen*.

Watchmen has often been referred to as the "*Citizen Kane* of comics." The comparison is apt. There are many similarities between *Kane* and *Watchmen*: both rely on heavy use of flashbacks from multiple viewpoints, parallels, and juxtapositions of word and image to tell stories set in motion by a death and gradually exposing a momentous secret.

Nearly 70 years after its release, *Kane* still routinely tops lists of the greatest films of all time, from organizations as cutting edge as *Cahiers du Cinema* to the more staid and traditional American Film Institute. The unparalleled critical standing of *Citizen Kane* is not primarily due to its story, nor the audience's identification with any of the characters, but is mostly due to the virtuosic way in which the story is told. *Kane* redefined how the medium of film could be used, and its chronologically displaced structure and astounding cinematography still feel ahead of the curve.

Like *Kane*, *Watchmen* may well still top lists of the best comics of all time 70 years after its release. And like *Kane*, *Watchmen* is so impeccably constructed that what lingers more than any specific narrative point is the precisely detailed construction linking the entire work together. Moore and Gibbons put on a master class in storytelling methods only available in the comics medium.

When used properly, the juxtaposition of words and pictures reveals more than either element could on its own. *Watchmen* can be experienced as a linear story or as an artistic construction to be looked on as a purely aesthetic object. The symmetrical "mirror" structure of issue #5, for example, encourages this more aesthetic reading. The symmetry adds little to the narrative but provides an added layer of aesthetic interest for the reader. The myriad ways Moore and Gibbons used the medium made it seem as if virtually every other writer and artist out there were barely trying. The story of *Watchmen* is also effective and emotionally engaging, but what makes the work as a whole so special is not what happens but how those events are conveyed.

The idea of making a film of *Watchmen* seems inherently misguided on some level. The work's strength is its unique use of the comic-book medium. Would anyone care to read a novel of *Citizen Kane*? A painting of a Beatles song? But in our culture, there's a hierarchy of artistic media. Novels and comics will be optioned and ascend into "major motion pictures," as if film is the most powerful medium – and every other kind of work merely an audition for the eventual film. People read *Watchmen* and envisioned what the movie would be like. They imagined a dream film, faithful to the book in every way. When that movie finally arrived, it was a classic illustration of the need to be careful what you wish for.

In what may be a deliberate tip of the hat to *Citizen Kane*, a snow globe in Laurie's childhood memories indicates a lost moment of innocence. From *Watchmen* #9 (May 1987). Copyright © DC Comics.

As far back as 1989, producer Joel Silver had approached director Terry Gilliam about directing a *Watchmen* film. Deeming it "the *War and Peace* of comics," Gilliam set to work on the project... and ultimately decided that a single film couldn't do justice to the material. Darren Aronofsky and Paul Greengrass were also rumored to be connected with the project at various times. *Watchmen* was finally brought to the screen by Zack Snyder immediately following his 2007 film version of *300*, adapted from the graphic novel by Frank Miller and noted for its extreme fidelity to the source material.

The density of *Watchmen* encourages rereading more than the average comic book or graphic novel. You can get the story on the first go, but it's a totally different experience on the second or third read. Reading it so many times gives the reader a very specific and ingrained understanding of the work – and great recall for individual lines and images.

That's what made watching the film such a surreal experience. Unlike previous adaptations from the work of Alan Moore such as the dire *League of Extraordinary Gentlemen*, there aren't that many glaring alterations to the text in *Watchmen*. What we see on screen is *Watchmen*. The story is there, and as the film progressed, I could practically sense the pages flipping as images marking the beginning of chapters appeared on screen. I always had a sense of where we were in the book, and I recognized many of the lines being spoken as direct quotations from the text. Many scenes were captured on screen with a reverent faithfulness rarely seen in cinematic adaptation. Tiny details in the background of the film called back to moments from the comic, and even details you wouldn't expect to see in a mainstream film – Doctor Manhattan's penis, say – made it to the screen.

In many ways, this is the adaptation fans dreamed of seeing. It's dark and moody, not shying away from the moral ambiguity and heavy adult sensibility of the comic. An R-rated super-hero movie budgeted at $130 million, featuring among other things recurrent male full frontal nudity and the destruction of New York City echoing the events of 9/11. To have such a film greenlit by a major studio, produced, filmed, and promoted so heavily – wasn't that the goal? Many people had hoped that *Watchmen* the movie could do for super-hero movies what *Watchmen* the comic did for super-hero comics: opening up a new age of more complex, mature films. So why did the film wind up being such an unexceptional, bizarrely disconnected viewing experience?

Answering that question requires a journey to the core appeal of *Watchmen*. Is it the deconstruction of super-heroes? Is it the meticulously arranged narrative style? Or is its rarefied status due to the confluence of all these into an almost flawless single-volume work? Watching the movie makes it clear that the stylistic tricks don't exist merely to show off: they enhance our immersion in the narrative, and consequently enhance the emotional experience of the work. You can't split up the pieces of *Watchmen* because they all reflect on each other to create a uniquely powerful piece of fiction.

Perhaps the most uniquely comic book aspect of the work is the comic within a comic that underscores significant portions of the action. "Tales of the Black Freighter" serves many roles: it's an ironic commentary on the action, humorously juxtaposed against the lengthy monologues of Bernard the news vendor. It also builds the world of the story by showing us what comics would be like in a world where super-heroes are real.

Reading *Watchmen*, I sometimes get a bit annoyed with the lengthy purple prose-captioned excerpts from the Black Freighter story. Even as I respect all the interesting visual and dialogue juxtapositions, it can reach the point where I just want to get on with things. Without any direct connection to the narrative, it seems like prime material to cut from a film adaptation. But in many ways, it's the key to the success of the entire work. Because *Watchmen* is so intricately constructed, pulling out any piece lessens the experience of the whole.

Over the course of the book, Moore and Gibbons build a cross-section of humanity around an intersection in New York City, filled with supporting characters that become lodged in your memory. For example, the psychiatrist Malcolm Long is central to Chapter VI, but he doesn't disappear from the book afterwards. The marital conflict between Long and his wife in that chapter, seemingly a device to show how Rorschach's psychosis is so great that it infects anyone he comes in contact with, turns out to have a purpose all its own. Moore gives Dr. Long his own emotional payoff, when Malcolm and his wife almost reconcile, but give up after Malcolm can't help but try to break up a street fight between Joey the taxi driver and her partner Aline, both of whom we've also seen recurring throughout the book. Pretty much each character with a speaking part in the book has his or her own little fully-realized arc. Snyder's film can recreate all the little details of the setting – give or take an electric car or redesigned cigarette along the way – and those are important, but what really makes the world of *Watchmen* special is the characters that inhabit it, and he can't give us that level of detail.

The aforementioned scene with Dr. Long is also significant as representation of Doctor Manhattan's revelation about the inherently chaotic and evolving world of humanity. On Mars, Jon realizes that the sheer number of coincidences and events it took to create Laurie, or any human, makes every human a kind of miracle. The astronomical chances against any person coming into being give him a new appreciation for the everyday travails of a world from which he'd grown distant. What hand shapes the universe to ensure that thousands of years of events occur to bring each individual person into existence?

In the course of the comic, we see what leads Dr. Long and his wife to that intersection. We see what leads Joey and Aline to be there. We see their paths converging with Bernard the news vendor. By seeing all the individual pieces that lead up to the confrontation on the street, we see things from Dr. Manhattan's perspective, or perhaps God's perspective – understanding how thousands of choices from many disparate people lead to the creation of each moment. In this case, a thematic point from the A story is illustrated and reinforced through the events of the B story.

There's a great debate in the work about the nature of humanity. The sterling reputations of the wartime heroes are revealed to be a cover for various forms of depravity, chronicled in Hollis Mason's book. The next generation of heroes is caught up in their own issues. Readers seize on characters like Rorschach or the nihilistic Comedian as evidence of Moore's dark view of humanity and heroism. Moore has taken symbols of justice and good like Superman and Batman and warped them into the aloof, inhuman Dr. Manhattan, the depraved Rorschach, or the pathetic Nite Owl. Even the heroes that our culture aspires to are nothing more than a bundle of psychiatric detritus, using the excuse of "doing good" as a way of satisfying their own desires. In such a world, it would seem, there are no heroes.

But as the world falls apart around them, ordinary people don't splinter into fear and turn on each other. On the streets by the newsstand, we see a disparate bunch of strangers come together to break up a fight, to help each other. Malcolm tries to help a stranger even though it might mean the loss of his marriage. After all the heroic posturing of the Crimebusters and Minutemen, this is a moment of selfless reaching out to another human being.

All the "heroes" are so caught up in the gadgets and the costumes that they forget what being a hero is actually about. The people on the street revert to their base instinct... and it turns out their base instinct is not to hurt each other, but to help each other. As Veidt's weapon arrives in New York, we don't see selfishness; we see Bernard the news vendor reach out to shield young Bernard. In his last moment, the cynicism we've heard nonstop from Bernard disappears, and his final act is an attempt to save someone else, someone he barely knows.

In the book's final chapter, we view a series of full-page spreads looking at the destruction wrought by Veidt's plan. We see the bodies of characters we knew stacked high and bloody on the streets. Seeing the full extent of the violence, of characters we know dead, is what makes the ending so much more visceral than the typical destruction of landmarks in countless summer blockbusters.

It's this glimpse at the destruction combined with our connection to the characters that makes the debate at the end much more than an abstract intellectual discussion. Objectively, what Veidt says makes sense: it is too late to make a difference, and exposing his plot would only throw things into chaos. But at the same time, the emotional impact of all that death is hard to take. We need some kind of justice, and Rorschach incarnates that desire. We may be repulsed by him at times throughout the narrative, but when we read those final pages, we empathize with him – rooting for him to make it back to the mainland and expose what happened. His death is one of the most wrenching in the story, yet another sacrifice in pursuit of Veidt's utopia.

But in the words of the German author Kurt Tucholsky that are usually attributed to Joseph Stalin, "One death is a tragedy, a million is a statistic." In the film, the moral conundrum loses much of its punch, and thus the ending becomes a purely intellectual exercise, instead of an emotional one. The central difference is the absence of the ancillary street characters in the film. Some of those scenes were likely filmed for restoration in a director's cut... but a film must ultimately be judged on what actually appears on screen, and those scenes, those emotional beats, were not there. Without the street life, we have no particular emotional investment in the destruction in New York.

And without that, it becomes the same urban destruction we've seen in countless other movies. They could say that every single person in the universe was wiped out; above a certain level it's just numbers. This problem is magnified by the fact that Laurie and Dr. Manhattan don't venture down onto the streets, as they do in the comic. They look at the damage from far away, focusing on the destroyed property, not the bodies. As such, neither they nor the audience ever really feel the impact of what Veidt did, and thus we don't feel the emotions the ending wants us to feel.

The changes to the end in the film – using the Dr. Manhattan's energy instead of the "squid" from the comic – are of debatable merit. Either way, the device is a MacGuffin: something designed to move the characters into the moral conundrum demanded by the ending. But the film's ending seems more arbitrary, largely because the groundwork for it hasn't really been laid. The pirate comic, besides functioning as an ironic counterpoint to the street scenes, lays the groundwork for the moral conundrum of the ending. The Black Freighter is Moore's comment on the inevitable failure of Veidt's plan: a man riding on a raft of bodies to a utopia he'll never reach. Veidt imagines his utopia, but we've already seen how good intentions can go horribly awry and lead only to pain.

Without the Black Freighter story, we don't have the grounding for the sort of moral questions raised by the ending. Even if only subconsciously, the pirate story raises those issues – and also provides one of the most illuminating pieces of the re-reading experience, when you realize how that whole story is really a comment on the ending itself. Cutting the pirate comic deprives the story of one of its most sophisticated layers, and guts the ending of its emotional and intellectual core. Without the development of the New York street world, the film feels more hermetically sealed, less about building an entire universe and more about just telling a super-hero story.

Now, this isn't entirely the fault of the film. Being a lengthy comic, serialized in chapters, *Watchmen* had the freedom to go deeper into character and spend time with side plots like the news vendor. Moore has mentioned that the series was originally planned for six issues, and when it expanded to 12, he filled in the gaps with the character pieces and side elements, like the pirate comic. The comic will be read in multiple sittings, with breaks. A film is meant to be experienced in one go, and that means that it needs to have a more linear narrative without excess digressions.

And this is where watching the film can be truly illuminating. The film does an incredible job of replicating the majority of the *Watchmen* comic on screen; I don't think anyone but the most pedantic fan could fault it for faithfulness to the source. Yes, the film deletes a lot, but what it presents is extremely faithful, with Snyder treating the published comic almost like his storyboards, just as he had previously done with Frank Miller's *300*. The film is an almost surreal experience because it's so close, yet also totally devoid of what makes *Watchmen* the comic so brilliant. Shouldn't a film that so closely replicates the story content of the "greatest comic book of all time" at least be a good movie? I find it impossible to assess the film with a typical thumbs up / thumbs down dichotomy because the film's total fidelity makes it impossible to look at, outside the context of the source material. Where does the film end and where does the book begin? That closeness magnifies the changes that were made, so that they jump out more than in most comic-book adaptations.

Even "Tales of the Black Freighter" was produced as a separately-released DVD, along with a mock television "news report" about Hollis Mason's "Under the Hood." The DVD is targeted only at the most hardcore fans; people who've seen the film but haven't read the book would have no clue why this pirate story exists. Though I admire Snyder for wanting to be thorough and tell the story, watching "Black Freighter" out of context is an even more hollow experience than the *Watchmen* film. The pirate comic exists as a commentary on the main narrative through ironic juxtaposition of its narrative and Veidt's, and the specific captions and images of the comic with the events on the street at any given time. Taken out of that context, it became just a pirate story with an overwrought narration. (An "Ultimate Cut" DVD incorporating the "Black Freighter" material into the narrative as it had appeared in the comic was released in November 2009, eight months later.)

A lot of what makes *Watchmen* so popular, particularly among casual comic-book readers, is its self-contained nature. The vast majority of super-hero comics take place in the convoluted world of the DC or Marvel Universe. Even something like Moore's *Swamp Thing* or Neil Gaiman's *Sandman* draw on DC Comics history in a way that could confuse new readers. By contrast, there are no other *Watchmen* comic stories; the entire world is contained in that single volume.

In that sense, *Watchmen* isn't comparable to most comic-book adaptations or any prior super-hero movie, because it's an adaptation of one specific work. It's closer to an adaptation of a novel than something like the Batman films directed by Tim Burton or Christopher Nolan. Those films drew on 70 years of stories, and a general perception of a character, not on one specific narrative. Which Batman film is "most faithful" to the comics: the 1966 *Batman*, the 1989

Batman, or the 2005 *Batman Begins*? Evidence can be found to support the idea that any of these is the most accurate. While the *Watchmen* characters are more specific characters in a specific narrative, Batman is a multifaceted figure in cultural mythology. Batman's story is inherently without an ending; even the most celebrated attempt to create a "last" Batman story, Frank Miller's *The Dark Knight Returns,* had a sequel.

(That's also a large part of why the *Watchmen* book enjoyed such a sales boost as buzz surrounding the film began to grow. If you want to read a Wolverine comic, there are literally hundreds to choose from; given the ongoing serialized nature of comics, none of them is the definitive Wolverine comic. With *Watchmen,* there's only the one book.)

Watching the *Watchmen* film, I marveled at the meticulous universe constructed on screen. Countless minor details had no impact on the narrative but helped immerse you in the world the comic had created. But the narrative felt lifeless next to the vital, emotional landscape of the comic. The film couldn't help but feel like a second-generation copy. And that prompted me to think about the relative successes and failures of the movie. I love the fact that they paid so much attention to building a credible world on screen, but wouldn't that effort have been better served in the creation of something new? *Watchmen* is a great story, but just retelling that story on screen doesn't add anything new to our world. In his more recent work, Alan Moore often focuses on the connection between storytellers and magicians. Both work to create something out of nothing. What kind of magic act is it to simply do the same exact thing that someone did before, only not as good?

In talking about his reasons for making the *Watchmen* film, Zach Snyder focuses almost entirely on his love of the original work and his desire to make an ultra-faithful adaptation, a "present for the fans." In a similar way to the lifeless Xerox film adaptation of *Sin City*, the *Watchmen* movie fails because its primary reason to exist is for the director to tell people that he liked this comic book.

What if Snyder had been placed in the same position as Moore was, when he originally pitched the series as a showcase for the Charlton super-heroes, and was told to do something original instead? Would Snyder have put all the world-building effort into telling a new story with as great a scope as the *Watchmen* film? Separated from its connection to the comic, the film is something to marvel at, spanning decades of history and going from Earth to

Mars. It's a huge work, and very rarely will you see a film with so high a budget granted the latitude to engage in a myriad of heavy philosophical themes. Snyder invested the time needed to build that world because he wanted to be faithful to the comic, but I was left wondering why more films don't do that kind of world-building. The short answer is because they don't need to. Moore and Gibbons didn't need to build that whole world to tell their super-hero story either. But in doing so, they made a great story into an all-time classic. The lesson of the *Watchmen* film is not to slavishly cling to your source material, trying to replicate it in every way, but to take the lessons of what worked about the original – the ambitious world-building and meticulous network of characters – and adapt that to a new story that could build on those themes and bring in something more personal.

In recent years, Alan Moore has tended to distance himself from *Watchmen* as a kind of adolescent work, but it shares many of the thematic concerns that underlie his more recent series such as *Promethea* or *The League of Extraordinary Gentlemen*. There's a personal, emotional investment in the work that just can't exist for someone whose primary goal is to replicate something he read as a teenager. Moore has often criticized the super-hero works that arose in the wake of *Watchmen*, claiming that *Watchmen* was used as an excuse for grown men to keep reading the characters they grew up with, without shame, and for writers to fuse their adult appetites for sex and violence with the fantasy characters they loved as children. One may argue this is hypocritical from a man who wrote a lengthy pornographic novel about characters from *Peter Pan*, *Alice in Wonderland*, and *The Wizard of Oz*, but his general point remains relevant, particularly to the *Watchmen* film. When Moore deconstructed the super-hero with *Watchmen* and *Miracleman*, it was about using the hero as a way to explore social concerns of the time – and general truths about the human condition. Many of the "grim and gritty" late-'80s and early-'90s super-hero works clearly weren't about anything other than just violence for the sake of violence.

Snyder's *Watchmen* film exists to try and recapture the experience of reading *Watchmen* for the first time. The film has nothing new to say, and exists primarily as a nearly three-hour advertisement for its source material. Moore wasn't reworking the Charlton characters or Miracleman solely because he loved the characters; he saw them as a device to explore his personal thematic concerns. Perhaps whoever made the *Watchmen* film should have adapted it to his or her own interests in the same way. The great irony is that Snyder made a love letter to Moore's work which was totally rejected by Moore, loudly and publicly at every opportunity.

A couple of months after the film's release, it had largely vanished from the cultural dialogue. It had a huge opening weekend, taking in $55 million, but its box office eroded quickly after that. The release of the direct to DVD *Tales of the Black Freighter* barely made an impact. It turned out the worst thing the film adaptation of *Watchmen* could do for itself was actually be released. Sales of the book skyrocketed from the moment the adaptation was announced, then jumped another level when the trailer made its debut in front of *The Dark Knight*. The promise of another mature super-hero epic to follow up the beloved Batman sequel had people chomping at the bit, and many seemed almost obligated to check out the book that would lead to what surely would be one of the biggest films of 2009. People read *Watchmen* on the subway; it was displayed prominently in bookstores. *Watchmen* had arrived, and surely the film would only take it to an even higher level. But the actual release of the film was an anti-climax. It drew neither the venom of a *League of Extraordinary Gentlemen* nor the acclaim of *The Dark Knight*. It was just sort of there.

Ultimately, for me at least, the release of that first trailer was the film's high point. Having read the book, I already knew the story of *Watchmen*. Nothing in the film itself was any particular surprise. The only real appeal was the novelty of seeing the characters move, of seeing the film's reality up on screen, and I got all that from the trailer. Though I have no particular affection for the final film, seeing that trailer for the first time was a great experience. A series of moving images juxtaposed with music: that's the one thing that *Watchmen* the comic couldn't do.

But once the novelty was gone, we were left with an adaptation that had all the surface but none of the soul. In time, the film adaptation will become a cultural footnote, while the book itself will continue to be read and discussed for years to come.

A Fellowship of Legendary Beings: About the Contributors

Richard Bensam has worked in the comics industry for a variety of publishers as a writer, editor, and graphic designer. He was also a contributor to the anthology *Teenagers from the Future: Essays on the Legion of Super-Heroes*, also from Sequart Research and Literacy Organization. Richard lives in New York City and blogs at estoreal.blogspot.com.

Mary Borsellino is an Australian writer and general troublemaker. When she was younger, Mary thought she'd grow up to write science fiction novels, but that hasn't happened yet. She also wanted to be a doctor, a hairdresser, a police officer, or a brave wanderer who had adventures. She's managed the latter, but the others are looking increasingly unlikely as time goes on. Her non-fiction and academic writing can be found at monkeywench.net and her trashy vampire novels at thewolfhouse.net.

Timothy Callahan is a writer, educator, husband, and father of two amazing children. He is the author of *Grant Morrison: The Early Years* and the editor of *Teenagers from the Future: Essays on the Legion of Super-Heroes* (both from Sequart). He blogs about comic books and pop culture at geniusboyfiremelon.blogspot.com.

Jon Cormier lives and works in Ottawa, Ontario. He spends more time thinking about comics than writing and (infrequently) maintains a blog at hypnoray.blogspot.com.

Julian Darius holds a Ph.D. in English and an M.A. in French. He founded Sequart Research and Literacy Organization, for which he wrote *Classics on Infinite Earths: The Justice League and DC Crossover Canon*, *Improving the Foundations: Batman Begins from Comics to Screen*, and a lengthy essay in *Teenagers from the Future: Essays on the Legion of Super-Heroes*. He has also authored fiction and non-fiction unrelated to comics.

Walter Hudsick is a longtime comic-book reader, former insurance bureaucrat, former police detective, former library clerk, former neighborhood advocate, former safety director, and current college rhetoric instructor who regularly uses comics in his classroom (and thus will the circle be unbroken, bye and bye). He lives in Seattle and blogs about comics at ninthart.blogspot.com.

Geoff Klock has a doctorate from Oxford University, where he studied at Balliol College. He is the author of two academic books, *Imaginary Biographies* and *How to Read Superhero Comics and Why*. He hosted a discussion at the Metropolitan Museum of Art with creators involved with the Iron Man and X-Men films, and writer Matt Fraction named a villain after him – the killer Dokkktor Klockhammer. He is an assistant professor at Borough of Manhattan Community College. Geoff blogs at geoffklock.blogspot.com.

John Loyd is a journalist residing in Western New York. He earned his B.A. in Communication from Roberts Wesleyan College (Rochester, NY). He has had work published by *The Democrat & Chronicle* in Rochester, NY, and *The Batavia Daily News*. He has also published freelance work for Mellon & Co. In 2008, he was a panel speaker at the Eastern Communication Association conference (Pittsburgh, PA), where he presented on the comic-book medium and *Watchmen*. He currently works as a reporter for *The Olean Times Herald*.

Patrick Meaney is a writer, director, producer, film editor, and a cofounder of Respect! Films. The author of *Our Sentence is Up: Seeing Grant Morrison's The Invisibles* (also published by Sequart), Patrick is currently producing and directing feature-length documentaries on comics, including *Grant Morrison: Talking with Gods* (see grantmorrisonmovie.com). Patrick also writes and directs the web serial *The Third Age*, which can be seen at thethirdagebegins.com. Patrick blogs at thoughtsonstuff.blogspot.com.

Chad Nevett has a B.A. in English and political science and an M.A. in English Language & Literature / Creative Writing. He resides in Windsor, Ontario. Chad does reviews online for the news site Comic Book Resources, blogs for Comics Should be Good, writes about wrestling for 411mania, and maintains his own blog at graphicontent.blogspot.com.

Gene Phillips grew up in the Silver Age of Comics but this has so far not had any undue silvering effects on his hair. He's written for most of the better-known comics zines and is currently working on a book project about the Fantastic Four. He blogs about myth, literature, and comics at arche-arc.blogspot.com.

William Ritchie studied the History and Philosophy of Science at the University of British Columbia with the late Stephen M. Straker, Ph.D., igniting a lifelong passion for this relatively new, important interdisciplinary field. A chronically underemployed writer, William resides in Vancouver, blogs pseudonymously on the internet, and is also available at reasonable rates to paint your fence.

Peter Sanderson is a comic-book critic and historian, as well as a lecturer on the study of graphic novels as literature. Early in his career, he served as the first and only Official Archivist of Marvel Comics. Since then, Peter has authored a number of books, taught the class "The Graphic Novel as Literature" at New York University, has curated exhibitions for the Museum of Comic and Cartoon Art, and reviews the latest in comics and comics-related material for *Publishers Weekly*. His online column *Comics in Context* can be found at asitecalledfred.com/category/comics-in-context.

Also from Sequart

CLASSICS ON INFINITE EARTHS: THE JUSTICE LEAGUE AND DC CROSSOVER CANON / by Julian Darius / forthcoming

OUR SENTENCE IS UP: SEEING GRANT MORRISON'S *THE INVISIBLES* / by Patrick Meaney, introduction by Timothy Callahan, Grant Morrison interview / 356p / $19.99

GRANT MORRISON: THE EARLY YEARS / by Timothy Callahan, foreword by Jason Aaron, Grant Morrison interview / 280p / $15.95

IMPROVING THE FOUNDATIONS: *BATMAN BEGINS* FROM COMICS TO SCREEN / by Julian Darius / 264p / $14.99

TEENAGERS FROM THE FUTURE: ESSAYS ON THE LEGION OF SUPER-HEROES / edited by Timothy Callahan, foreword by Matt Fraction, afterword by Barry Lyga / 340p / $19.99

KEEPING THE WORLD STRANGE: A *PLANETARY* GUIDE / edited by Cody Walker / 180p / $11.99

GOTHAM CITY 14 MILES: 14 ESSAYS ON WHY THE 1960S BATMAN TV SERIES MATTERS / edited by Jim Beard, afterword by Jeff Rovin / 296p / $15.99

MUTANT CINEMA: THE X-MEN TRILOGY FROM COMICS TO SCREEN / by Thomas J. McLean / 296p / $15.95

For more information and for exclusive content, visit Sequart.org.

CPSIA information can be obtained at www.ICGtesting.com
Printed in the USA
LVOW08s0235131213

365058LV00001B/29/P